TAP THE HIDDEN POWER WITHIN YOU

Perspectives of an Overseas Filipino Worker

TAP THE HIDDEN POWER WITHIN YOU

Perspectives of an Overseas Filipino Worker

Authored by

Engr. Eva Magalay Barientos

Disclaimer

This book has been published with all reasonable efforts taken to make the material error-free after the consent of the author. This book is sold subject to the condition that it shall not, by way of trade or otherwise, be lent, resold, or otherwise circulated without the copyright owner's prior written consent in any form of binding or cover other than that in which it is published and without a similar condition including this condition being imposed on the subsequent purchaser and without limiting the rights under copyright reserved above, no part of this publication maybe reproduced, stored in or introduced into a retrieval system or transmitted in any form or by any other means without the permission of the copyright owner.

Registered Office- 907-Sneh Nagar, Sapna Sangeeta Road,
Agrasen Square, Indore – 452001 (M.P.), India
Website: http://www.wingspublication.com
Email: mybook@wingspublication.com

First Published by WINGS PUBLICATION 2024
Copyright **Engr. Eva Magalay Barientos** 2024

Title: **TAP THE HIDDEN POWER WITHIN YOU**
Price: AED 60 & $ 17
All Rights Reserved.
ISBN 978-93-6006-225-5

LIMITS OF LIABILITY/DISCLAIMER OF WARRANTY

Content

Dedication

This book exemplifies my profound gratitude and sincere appreciation to my greatest fortunes in life. To my husband Christopher E. Barientos, to my daughter, Christine Eve M. Barientos, and to all my family members – Magalay family and Barientos family.

This endeavour is also in loving memory and to honor my deceased parents, whose life's lessons, values, hard work and treasured moments continue to live on in our family.

Thank you for your unceasing support and unconditional love.

They truly inspire me to pursue this dream.

Above all, to God be all the glory for all the blessings, and making this dream a reality.

Acknowledgement

My heart is full of gratitude as I journey through life. I would never be where I am today if not for God's providence. All those have significantly contributed to my life.

This book would not have been possible without God's blessings, guidance and provisions. My overpowering gratitude to God for making things possible, despite some trials, for always being there to remind how blessed I am with His protection, talents and loving embrace. For giving me the right people who have been instrumental in my journey in fulfilling my dream as an Author.

Thank you, my immediate family and other family members who always have my back and who have wholeheartedly supported me every step of the way and in all my endeavours. They are my "knight in shining armour" for giving me unconditional love and understanding. You are truly a treasure that will forever be dearly preserved in my heart.

Thanks to my venerable mentors, my valued teachers and my advisers in life. You have inculcated in me invaluable guidance and teachings to mould my life in the right way and always encouraged me to believe in my capabilities. They are instrumental in providing me the driving force to soar high and reach greater heights.

Thanks to all those who have extended unwavering support and helped me in my education when my family and I needed it the most. You have been instrumental in paving the way for me to achieve my dreams.

Thanks to my friends, family friends, relatives, OFW friends and colleagues for your genuine support and encouragement, to take this courage to unleash my potential in the writing arena. Your kind words and motivation have ignited that ember of hope to hone my ability and be able to showcase my God-given talent in the hope of creating an impact to other people's lives.

Thanks to my niece Ara, for the support and being the trusted ally in times of distresses. Thanks also to my book writing classmate and friend Daisy, for the encouragement, advices and in lifting each other especially when we had writer's block.

My journey in completing this book was quite challenging. Thanks to a prolific Author and Coach - Dr. Kailash Pinjani, for providing invaluable guidance, motivation and trust in my capabilities. Thanks also to his Wings Publication International team for the expertise in the overall technical aspects of book publishing.

To all those who have silently and explicitly prayed for me and my family. For all those and more, I say - THANK YOU SO MUCH. You have been and always will be a part of me and my success.

Preface

Every day, as we journey through life, we are confronted with many trials and tribulations. We face challenges in terms of personal, emotional, psychological, financial, spiritual as well as other aspects of life. Each of us have chosen unique path in order to survive. As we take on the challenge, we make difficult decisions that would certainly test our strength and survival instincts. Mountain of problems and trials can be experienced by anyone at any given time.

More so in the life of the thousands of Filipino migrant workers like me. Those Overseas Filipino Workers (OFWs) who have chosen a challenging life in the aim of making a difference in the lives of their families. With the end goal of improving our life, there comes insurmountable stumbling blocks that we conscientiously confront head on for a greater purpose of achieving our dreams.

If you happen to read this book, then there is a possibility that either you're in the same predicament as mine, you have some family working in a foreign land or someone who shares the same interest in understanding the plight of OFWs. It is not by accident that you possess my book. There is a reason enough to transcend my perspectives on how I have successfully hurdled adversities and insurmountable difficulties in the rocky road I have taken in the pursuit of making a difference in the life of my family and creating benefits for others.

Overcoming obstacles is not easy. We are already among the men and women who have toiled selfless sacrifices and we have to stay on course with a positive and resilient mindset, continually moving forward towards the realization of our dreams.

I fervently hope that after reading this book, you will feel empowered and inspired, realizing that all of us have that inner power to continually believe in the greater Divine power, making all things possible for us to survive and succeed in life. Wherever you are and whatever you do in your chosen field, please remind yourself through self-introspection that you will never give up in the face of adversity.

We need to be strong and we have to stand firm in our decision to have taken this unique and tough route. If we want to achieve our dreams, sacrifices have to be made. Amidst all the misfortunes, if we painstakingly stay connected to our biggest WHY, then there is no doubt that we will reach our final destination in the fulfilment of our aspirations.

Are you an OFW? Or do you have an OFW family or friends? If you are struggling or you know anyone struggling for survival, then you are not alone. We are on a journey laden with trials and obstacles, yet we come out stronger. The concepts and perspectives I have presented in this book may be instrumental in stimulating inspiration to have a positive perspective in life. An inspiration that we don't have to look down on ourselves; we have to be proud that our heroic act of enduring poignant episodes has made us stronger to grapple with the many challenges in our quest to improve our lives.

Gifted with different talents, knowledge and skills, success is within reach at our own pace and with God's grace, we are now starting to realize our dreams. Personally, I have been into countless problems and impediments in life. Having been born and raised in a remote area with meagre resources, my parents brought me up, inculcating the importance of prayer, determination, right attitude and education as game-changers in improving life's situation.

Since I was young, I have been exposed to many hardships and challenging situations. Money and resources were scarce and not within reach to have that comfortable life. But my parents instilled in me the lessons from hardships. Those lessons have been the significant building blocks in developing perseverance, discipline, and hard work to connect to my purpose in life continually. My education has been instrumental in the practical implementation of what I have learned in real life.

Although, I still stumble and fall, but I have realized that I have the basic ingredients to survive this life and come out as a better person with God's guidance and my family as my anchor and tangible inspiration.

It is my dream to touch other people's life, to create an impact in the hope that I can propagate positivity especially for those who are having struggles and tough times. For the thousands of OFWs and their families, may we begin to realize that we are a precious and selfless human being. Within our inner core, we have that power to understand ourselves through introspection and meditation in knowing our true value and purpose in life.

Despite the many storms in our lives, from separation anxiety to financial challenges and many others, we can emerge victorious for as long as we know how to embrace a positive and resilient mindset. It comes with grit in managing our emotions effectively and successfully overcoming stress and depression.

It cannot be denied that one of the reasons we work abroad is to look for opportunities to improve our financial situation. And in this book, you can draw some tips and motivation to enhance financial literacy, continually making goals and growing through continuous learning and professional development. It is my prayer that I can convey positivity and hopefully you can embrace an optimistic mindset and continue to believe in yourself, that no matter what happens you have to move forward.

I have been to many depressing situations, too. There may be times that we think we are powerless in our lowest moments and defeats. But I have realized that there is no greater power than unleashing our hidden power to connect to that greater Divine power for us to get stronger and bolder, for us to never give up and continually work towards the realization of our dreams.

It is my wish that you will be able to read my book, digest it and relate it with your own life's experiences as well. With humility and compassion, I hope and pray that my way of expressing my experiences and perspectives, will inspire you to become better versions of yourselves.

Word from Author

In the path that I have taken, it comes with consequences – both adverse and beneficial. But I have survived, conquered my fears and limiting beliefs, hurdled obstacles and embody positivity in gradually changing my perspective in life for the better.

I have written this book with the genuine intention to inspire those who have relatable experiences especially in the life of OFWs. It is based on my personal perspectives and citing some real examples from my actual encounters.

As you read and flip through the pages of this book, it is my earnest hope and prayer that you will have an open mind. I don't mean to cause any offense, awkward feeling and discomfort to anyone. I just want to share the valuable lessons based on generally practiced principles that I have implemented in my life, as I journey towards the realization of my dreams.

Whatever challenges you may be facing right now, don't get discouraged, and never give up on your dreams. Stay connected with the Divine power throughout your journey. Feel free to connect with me and together we can create a community of positivity and optimism as we marvel in pursuing this path to success towards a happy and fulfilled life that we rightfully deserve.

Engr. Eva Magalay Barientos

UNDERSTANDING YOURSELF

Whatever we do and wherever we are in this world, we are always busy dancing with the hustle and bustle of this thing called life. Most of the time, it gets very difficult to just slow down and take a mindful respite for re-evaluation of what we've gone through and where we are heading. And as we journey through life, there are countless stops and starts in trying to understand ourselves better.

Who Are You?

If we are given the chance to be in our solitude for a few hours, pausing from anything we do in this fast-paced and demanding world, what is that one question we might want to ask ourselves? Perhaps there are many questions that will emanate from our minds, and it would lead to more questions than answers. But if we try to reflect for a moment, maybe one question would be, Who Am I? This entails deeper rethinking and most of us would be left wondering how and why we ask this question. As we delve deeper at this point, maybe we don't really know the real answer.

Have you been in the same dilemma of asking yourself? Amidst the countless questions flooding our minds, that tiny echo of "Who Am I?" reverberates most profoundly deep within us. We are faced with many challenges in terms of work, emotions, finances, relationships and almost everything. And we rarely get the chance to self-evaluate as to where and how we fare in the life we have chosen. Personally, being an Overseas Filipino Worker (OFW) in the United Arab Emirates (UAE) for quite some time, I have gone through a journey laden with adversities and challenges that made the road seemingly difficult and unassailable on many occasions.

This question delves into the complexity within us and entails an exploration of discovering our true self. It may sound bizzarre, but self-introspection is also decoding our true identity and character. Its eccentricities may lead to enumerable mysteries in our inner selves. Deep within, we need to re-examine ourselves as to who we are and how well do we know ourselves. Because from time to time, we seem to question everything and if we don't have the answers, we seem to evade and reroute through several diversions.

It comes to self-introspection and from this we can develop more feelings as we throw this question deep inside us. We tend to reflect as to where we stand in life. As we try to dig deeper and deeper, so many things evolve and we try to look back, imagine the future and yet, not knowing and having that answer. When we are faced with many issues, complex questions start to unravel in our quest to understand our true selves.

But for every answer, there is another question, and self-exploration is very essential as it is a never-ending journey towards discovering our true selves in these challenging times.

Understanding Self-Esteem

Much has been said about self-esteem and theoretically we seem to understand it well. We encountered this word even when we were still in our university days but it is still difficult to comprehend how we implement it in real life scenarios.

What is self-esteem, then? According to Oxford Learner's Dictionaries *(https://www.oxfordlearnersdictionaries.com/)*, self-esteem is "a feeling of being happy with your own character and abilities". It is how we feel and look at ourselves and how we value our own strengths and weaknesses. It is a perception and feelings emanating from our own mind and it depends on how we view things from within. It is comparable to looking at ourselves and having the belief that we have good value and positive influence over others.

We can have high or low self-esteem. We have many experiences in life that test our self-esteem, and it can be likened to a gauge, sometimes high and sometimes low. It is all up to us to maintain a healthier level of self-esteem, which is essential as we brace with the many trials in life. For instance, when we are subjected to a competitive exercise, there may be times that we tend to be critical of our own capabilities, thus leading to low self-esteem. It can affect our performance as we tend to doubt if we have that innate power to excel and exhaust possibilities beyond comparison. This perception of being incapacitated, inept and not physically pleasing hampers our chances of winning in many aspects of life.

Having high self-esteem is an important ingredient in maintaining that confidence. In believing that no matter what, we can get through any hurdle and we stay on course without losing track of our health, emotional, relationships, professional and spiritual goals.

Building Self Confidence

There may be times when our self-confidence would be subjected to a test. We tend to question if we are confident enough to get through any endeavour in our career and personal life. It can be anything, such as speaking in public, writing an essay, taking an examination and many others. We are usually afraid to venture and try doing something because, by nature, we would be uttering the phrase - "I don't have self-confidence". And the power of this statement puts us in a limiting conviction because we doubt our capabilities. Indeed, self-doubt is an internal adversary of self-confidence.

So, how can we build self-confidence? By nature, many of us are not born confident, every skill we develop needs time to practice to eventually become adept in that area. We need to educate ourselves, develop our skills and enhance our arsenal to gain confidence and eradicate apprehension. If we try to focus on improving our lives, we can surely empower ourselves with the right learning attitude and consistency. Then, we can be confident in facing any challenges in life. We need time convincing ourselves that stepping out of our comfort zone is the first step to gradually wean from self-doubt.

This dilemma happens to anyone at any point in their career or personal life. In my early days as a Filipino expatriate in the UAE, I did not have that self-confidence during job interviews, and I had several job interview blunders. I have realized that adequate preparation, gaining knowledge, acquiring skills, learning from my mistakes and continually improving are essential ingredients to nail down that job interview and emerge as a successful applicant. Building self-confidence entails hard work and commitment to continually become better through constantly checking if we have slowly eliminated self-doubt.

Overcoming Insecurities

Many of us have our individual insecurities. It can be in physical appearance, in relationship, job performance, skills and talent and other aspects in our human existence. It is natural to feel insecure, but to live with it over a long period of time can bring us down and curtail our growth and opportunity to improve life as a whole. Insecurity starts with our thinking, and low self-esteem and self-doubt are preludes to making the insecurity reside within the fabric of our belief system.

Insecurity can shatter any chance to better our situation or derail any plan, but our mind has the power to overcome any insecurity if we try to look at it from a positive standpoint. We have to switch gears, thinking that we are not good enough, that we are not on par with others, and that we are less of a person compared to our peers. We cannot radiate positive vibrations unto others if we carry insecurity, even in hindsight. We need to slowly detach from the mental orientation that we are not enough and we lack something. It is a process of eliminating the negative spot in our mind and as we go through it, we may be able to unleash our potential. The first step might be difficult, but the further step can be easy if we start cleansing our minds. As a popular quote by Maya Angelou says - "The real difficulty is to overcome how you think about yourself."

I have a bunch of insecurities, too, like many of us. For example, my insecurity was put to a test when I was asked to be interviewed during a prestigious conference about Climate Change. At first, I refused for several reasons, and my inner voice was telling me that I wasn't good enough. With the insistence of the interviewer and as I was forced by circumstances, the interview went through, and I delivered the message well. This is a testament that we can always defeat our limiting mindset and we can break that barrier lurking in the corner of our mind to just let things flow naturally with confidence.

Believing in The Divine Power

A strong faith or belief system is very essential in our life. We need to believe. Believe in God, that all our prayers will be answered in His own perfect time, and keep in mind that He is the Creator who gives us strength to face the many difficult situations in life.

In our introspection, we discover that believing in God is the gateway to obtaining the strength and courage as we go through life. As we become feeble, seeking divine intervention and providence is necessary to relieve us of our maddening anxiety so we can move ahead into life with our greater purpose. We are nothing without Divine providence, we cannot be alone and need a strong spiritual anchor that prevents us from going adrift.

God's protection is a great assurance against difficult times, especially when we are at our lowest point. This can be attained by submitting ourselves through profound praying and reflection—no matter what happens, it is His will that shall prevail. This also gives us a chance to listen to our inner selves. When we are emotionally drained and worn out, pausing for some time in our solitude and reflecting on the positive things God has bestowed upon us can make us feel better through His enlightenment and comfort. It is through reflection and prayer that we can reinvigorate ourselves with the ultimate energy from above. In our solitary moments, we gradually unload our burden and cleanse our minds from negativities, and slowly create space for tranquillity to understand ourselves better.

As an OFW, I have that episode where I was defeated by the power of bad intention against me, and I was at my lowest point when I knew the devastation was connected to treachery, heartless action and unjustified exploitation, causing damage. But on that day, I prayed for God's power and the strength to carry on and regain what I had lost in due time.

Cultivating Belief in Yourself

There are days that when we wake up in the morning, we feel so sluggish and unmotivated to do anything, even just to move out from our bed. At this time, hope and exuberance seem to be elusive. And in those days, the predominant thought in our mind would be doubting ourselves and not believing that we can accomplish something. But if we don't believe in ourselves, then who else will? We cannot convince others to believe in us if we don't genuinely manifest it from deep within.

So, how do we remedy this internal chaos of self-doubt? There is no panacea or standard formula, but it starts from the moment we decide what strategy to implement and see if it works for us. No matter how we try to accessorize ourselves to display confidence, if we don't make a leapfrog from the negative instinct of self-doubt into igniting that energy to believe in ourselves, then perhaps we are just painting a façade, and we still dwell on doubting ourselves. It starts with a decision to instil a strong belief system in the inner self.

Harnessing that inner strength plays a crucial role in fueling our energy gauge at all times. We need not listen to that deafening whisper of negative compass to steal our enthusiasm. Believing in oneself is the essential trigger in our mind and kickstarts our body to move and feel confident that we are valuable with a purpose to fulfil.

From the perspective of being OFW, sometimes we need to break the barrier in our minds that makes us feel inferior to other people. There comes a time that necessitates us to be assertive and have the nerve to believe in our capabilities. We don't need to belittle and look down on ourselves. We just have to believe that we are also competitive and can excel in our chosen fields.

A strong belief system is not an overnight task but it entails continuous and consistent work. Some of the strategies we can try are connecting to the Divine power, enhancing our knowledge, upgrading ourselves, continually improving and getting ready by honing our skills and capabilities. Instead of being pessimistic, believe in yourself and have faith in your abilities. Believing in ourselves is also a reflection that we have a self-awareness of our own strengths, weaknesses and areas of improvement, realizing that we are always a work in progress.

Be Yourself and Break Free From Comparison

Even if we have a strong belief system, there comes a time that we are tempted to compare ourselves to others. In the end trying to emulate them and depart from our original self. We sometimes forget that being authentic is a powerful indicator that we know ourselves better and we are confident in the face of adversity and come out stronger.

We don't need to focus on our imperfections but embrace our frailties and have that self-awareness that we are a wonderfully unique creation with our own path to follow. We have to get away from the mentality of always comparing ourselves with others, instigating jealousy. Comparing ourselves to others can sometimes lead to a lackluster attitude, feeling timid and sleazy. This can result in undesirable behaviour when dealing with family, peers, and colleagues, as we become great pretenders, and people will find it difficult to trust us.

With the advent of social media, we need to be reminded that we use these platforms toward improving ourselves, gaining knowledge and not to keep on minding other people's business and then consequently compare ourselves with their status and achievements. When we are accustomed to comparison, we lose our identity, bearing its obstructive consequences on our personal growth. For instance, it is inevitable for some OFWs to compare with others in terms of economic, family, relationship and career achievements. But let us not forget that we have our own pacing and our unique opportunity that unfolds in God's perfect timing.

Being ourselves brings simplicity in accepting who we are without unnecessary pretensions, exaggerations and embellishments. It is better to look at others as inspiration to do better, breaking free from the shackles of comparison that we're lagging behind. Instead, we need to focus on life's blessings bestowed upon us, maintain that confidence and strong belief system aided with the right attitude at embracing our shortcomings and imperfections and staying on course with the direction we set to achieve our goals.

Embracing the Journey of Self-Discovery

Let us now take a moment and evaluate areas of our lives and reflect on how we know ourselves better today than yesterday. It would take us the long winding road to navigate to self-discovery, trying to decipher our answers to the many questions as we delve deeper. It requires an arduous exercise for reevaluating ourselves considering that knowing and understanding ourselves is never easy. But we need to acknowledge that discovering ourselves is a continual process.

As much as we want to understand ourselves, we have to prepare ourselves just like an empty cup ready to absorb personal breakthroughs. We may discover our behavioural patterns contrary to what we believe for the longest time. We may embrace change of hearts or manifest outlandish ideas and character, but it is truly an enriching journey.

In this daunting and reflective trail, we may discover more questions and compelling reasons to leverage answers in self-improvement, and persevering spirit is needed to never stop growing. We need to embrace that this is a giant step to fuel us in our daily life, encouraging a continuous exploration of ourselves as we stay on course knowing our purpose.

KNOWING YOUR PURPOSE

Do we really know our purpose in life? We may just wander and it seems obscure. It takes a considerable period of time to unleash that purpose. Knowing life's purpose, in general, is an essential compass to keep going as we traverse the path towards fulfilling our dreams and aspirations.

Defining Your Purpose

Defining our purpose is quite an enervating but worthwhile exercise. Let us take, for example, the case of OFWs. As migrant workers, when we decide to leave our country, we have differing viewpoints and apprehensions as we take on the difficult adventure of finding an opportunity in a foreign land. This is why we need an anchor, a strong connection to our purpose, that we leave our loved ones carrying unbearable sadness and precarious circumstances.

Being an OFW, knowing our purpose is very important. It plays a crucial role in providing direction to move forward and endure pain and desolation. Besides having inner motivation, it will also lead to a deeper sense of fulfilment despite the multitude of challenges and uncertainties associated with the path we choose to venture abroad.

So, what is your purpose? Many, if not all, may have the ultimate purpose of improving economically to provide our families with a better future while showcasing our talents in the global arena. Some may have the purpose of finding their career progression with the hope of meeting their dream guy or dream girl. Some may have the purpose of enriching themselves for a greater cause by supporting a charity. It is also possible that we left because there are limited opportunities for us to grow professionally, while some may just have the purpose of looking for a job while exploring the cultural diversity in a new country. Some of us may have a deeper sense of wanting to touch lives or create an impact in other people's lives. There can be enumerable purposes which can go on and on, varying from one person to another.

Defining our purpose serves as our fuel, possessing that burning desire to achieve what we want that can bring us fulfilment in life. Along the way in our journey, no matter how hard we try to segregate our concerns into compartments, we are constantly subjected to some trials that may abruptly dwindle our fighting spirit. Thus, it is very important to have definiteness in purpose to drive ourselves towards the right direction and not lose track of our purpose. We have to remind ourselves from time to time that we are doing this for a good cause, and it is not by accident that we are taking this path to make a difference in the lives of our families. We are not here for no reason; our existence has a purpose in creating value for other people.

Recognize Your Calling

When we pursue what we want, we reflect on our skills and capabilities and determine our passion to align our purpose with what we are called for, personally and professionally. There are those who started working in the field not of their own choice, but since it is the only opportunity at hand, there is no other option but to try. However, it is just a stepping stone to a vocation of your inclination that will give you ultimate fulfilment and happiness.

For instance, in my personal journey as an OFW, I have eventually found a career where I can practice my technical field while teaching others through training as part of the scope. And I find it fulfilling in the sense that I am given an opportunity to share my knowledge and guide others. I realize that it is not just happening accidentally, but it has a connection to my selfless character of sharing knowledge, while having an avenue to connect with my university experience in the Philippines in the field of teaching.

We have different calling and it does not necessarily mean that the opportunity is bestowed on us in the beginning. However, whatever we are called for in terms of vocation to serve others through our talents, knowledge and skills will surface eventually. If we have the calling for volunteerism, there are also avenues where we can serve in charitable works through various community groups.

Committing to Fulfill Your Purpose

Knowing what we want is one thing, but being committed to staying on track to fulfil it is another thing. This requires hard work, sacrifices and perseverance to stick with it at all costs. There comes a time when we will be subjected to troubling situations personally and professionally as we traverse through dreams and desires, which may result in us being exhausted and entertaining the idea of giving up. It requires our deep commitment, an untainted devotion with a firm decision that no matter what happens and what comes along in the face of any adversity, we need to reach our destination to achieve our goals.

Our profound dedication serves as our internal agreement with our inner self to stay connected with our purpose and not be dragged with negativities, losing the right track. If we are truly committed, no amount of discouragement can stop us from working consistently towards our goals. We may have some detours along the way, but commitment will bring us back to our senses and enable us to fulfil our purpose.

Why are we lost? Sometimes, we lose sight of our purpose, or we lack the commitment to fulfil our purpose as we journey through life. Let that commitment resonate within our inner core, and if we have 100% commitment, then we cannot be distracted in trying times. We may pause for a while, but there is a slim possibility of losing track. Personally, I have encountered some OFWs who have gone to their undesirable acts, proliferating their vices, enjoying life and who ended up losing their jobs, thus jeopardizing their future and that of their families. It is truly disheartening, but this is a reality we have to face and I'm sure several others see this unfortunate scenario within our community of Filipino migrant workers.

When we are lost, groping in the dark, then it necessitates us to see the light again and remind ourselves that we are here for a greater purpose. Or if we see others who are lost, then we have that obligation to be their inspiration to get back on their feet and compose themselves, bringing back that enthusiasm and burning desire to fulfil their dreams. It is never too late to extend a hand and get a lost individual back on track, traversing with lessons learned and possessing the ardour to persist until things become clearer towards the path to fulfilment.

Seeking Divine Guidance for Your Purpose

No matter how composed and determined we are, we still need a lot of energy to keep moving and staying on course. Whenever we are lost, we continuously search for that purpose when we introspect about where we are in our journey. And sometimes, we ask ourselves if we are really directed towards our purpose or if we are just getting astray and still hoping that someday the enlightenment will draw us to clarity in what we aspire for in our endeavours.

It is alright to have this predicament of confusion and having that insatiable mind. We are incessantly looking for answers as we go along, as we have that perseverance to pursue the search for our meaningful purpose. As part of our human nature, there are times we get easily swayed by minor issues that come our way, and we lose sight of where we are heading. We succumb to the temptation of detours and distractions, and we should keep a promise to ourselves that sacrifices have to be made as we steadily work things out.

It is inevitable to absorb negative thoughts no matter how empowered we are and how we attuned ourselves to committing to what we really want in life. From time to time, self-doubt would surface and contribute towards extinguishing our inner strength. When we are weary and downtrodden as if we are diverted from our true purpose, we cannot regain our energy alone.

The key is to never stop searching and never stop aspiring to be better versions of ourselves in comparison to our former self. And in this process, it essentially requires us to connect to the source - the Divine Power, seeking guidance for restoring the seemingly lost vivacity to go on. It is through the Divine Power that we are truly enlightened, with indomitable spirit in the face of adversity in our journey towards a purposeful life.

Propagating Humility

So, how do we maintain our alignment with the right purpose? Having determined and knowing fully well that we journey with a purpose does not preclude us from trying times. And we can create space to cultivate humility, knowing that our purpose is also a testament to our belief in the Divine Power. Humility in how we handle ourselves among our peers and being humble means realizing that everything is just temporary and that we need to be good stewards.

The process of knowing ourselves, our deep purpose, the wisdom to stay on course and the tenacity to hold on despite troubling situations can be attributed to Divine intervention. In anything, even if we have the abilities, talents and capabilities, staying humble is good trait. We should not be boastful and project ourselves with arrogance, oozing with over-confidence. Whatever we have, can also be taken away, just like any resource or possession in life. It necessitates us to be humble enough to acknowledge that we are nothing in this world if not for divine providence.

Being in difficult situations and surviving them is a humbling process. Our commitment and ability to withstand are put to the test when we are going through many obstacles in life. This makes us stronger in the process. The penultimate essence is that it grants us more humility to be subservient to the unpredictable nature of life, where confusion shows up anytime and anywhere. This is why we need to cultivate humility deep within us and radiate positive feelings to others.

With humility, we can also acknowledge our weaknesses and shortcomings. It simply means that every time we commit mistakes, we have to be humble enough to admit and ask for forgiveness for those whom we have hurt and caused some discomfort. Humility knows no boundary and has no requirements in terms of age and other attributes.

Overcoming Discouragement

Why do we get discouraged easily? For example, as OFWs, we are vulnerable to any form of depressing situation. As we try to filter all the negative feedback on our venture, the first instinct is that we may be discouraged and not confident to pursue it. Discouragement has a negative impact on our decisions and often causes confusion when taking on a challenge. This may happen to anyone for any reason that entertains negative comments from other people. The negative energy will pull us backwards and become an obstacle to achieving our goals in life.

So, we should not be acquiescent to other people's opinions. But we need to listen to our inner self with conviction and fervour to successfully attain what we have dreamed of. When we are confused, it requires reflection to reject negative thoughts and bring back positivity and optimism. If we keep entertaining the discouragement, it is not the spectators who will suffer the consequences of our distorted path and misdirection, but it is bouncing back on us. So why listen and be affected by undesirable comments if only to get distracted? After all, we are the sole in charge of life's purpose and we drive our own vehicle towards success.

This is my personal recollection of discouragement as an expatriate looking for a job in Dubai. At one point, I went through a grueling selection process for a post in a company and the interviewer seemed to be tough and unbending. As he went through my resume, he spotted something in my skills that "writing" is one. Then he told me, "You indicated that you can write well, now show me your English". This was his way to determine if I was telling the truth or just fabricating my resume. My first reaction was that I felt discouraged because the statement seemed to be derogatory and was already a distraction to my goal of being selected. And hearing that from a tough interviewer made me doubt my writing skill. I didn't have any other option, but I just reminded myself that I needed an entry-level job as a prelude to my engineering field. So, instead of being discouraged, I took a deep breath and wrote something on the spot. It is not to raise my own chair, but I was selected and aside from the technical aspect, I was assigned to check all communication coming out of the Construction Manager's office. After all, I have realized that if we don't give up, we can tap that hidden power within us to transform discouragement into an inspiration to achieve what we really want.

Connecting With A Purpose-Driven Community

There is always a community we can connect to. It can be an avenue to discover a group of people who can be a strong support system. Sometimes, when we let desolation and hopelessness take over, we cannot be alone and need a strong emotional support system to anchor us, preventing us from being lost.

A strong support system as a source of inspiration to move forward is an essential component of our fight against major adversaries and setbacks. As expats, we firmly believe that the betterment of our families is one of the main reasons for being away. And if we don't know our genuine purpose, we can connect with a purpose-driven community whose advocacy resembles what we believe in. Through this community, we don't feel separated and hopeless as it awakens our sensibility for deep reflection in life.

A community can also help us strengthen our faith and restore our belief system. It is not embarrassing to admit that we need help, we need other like-minded people in uplifting our "fighting spirit" to carry on in our quest to live a life with meaningful purpose. We don't have to limit our thinking that nobody cares because there are many amazing people ready to lend a hand if we only reach out with authenticity and genuine intention. We don't exist in isolation as social beings. We need to associate and connect with people, and through this connection, we can discover that our problems are nothing more than what others are going through.

With unity and a helping hand, we can feel that our existence is valuable and there is a reason why we are in the same predicament as others. Through community activities and volunteerism, we will have the chance to realize that we can still extend a helping hand despite the fact that we are also needing assistance. Helping people knows no border, as genuine concern for other people in need has no criteria. As human beings, we have that innate character of being kind. If you still don't know your purpose, connect with the right community and continue discovering your inner strength to carry on finding the true meaning of your existence.

Now, we have discovered our deep purpose. Our commitment is needed in staying connected with it every time we feel low in trying times. Know that there is the power of divine intervention that will guide us through, enabling gradual change in the way we ponder about life.

CHAPTER 3

MASTERING MINDSET

"Whatever the mind can conceive and believe, it can achieve."

~ Napoleon Hill

How powerful is our mind? What is mindset? Is it important? These are some powerful questions needed in setting the directions and framework on how strong and how frail we are in the pursuit of whatever we aspire for. *"A mindset is an established set of attitudes of a person or group concerning culture, values, philosophy, frame of mind, outlook, and disposition"*, taken verbatim from https://en.wikipedia.org/wiki/Mindset. Whether in personal, career, emotional or spiritual matters, our state of mind or the way we think is of paramount importance in our daily lives. Our frame of mind influences our actions. Perhaps we may have experienced that whatever is the predominant thought in our mind, it has the power to drag us into that state in terms of action, attitude and behaviour towards something.

Our mindset directs us in the course of implementing strategies and actions in order to achieve something. However, it is also a roadblock that hampers us to start. So, if we think we're weak, then we align to inaction, and our energy level deteriorates, leading us to just stare at nowhere, wondering when we can restore that energy to keep going. It has been said that "we are what we think".

Truly, this is a very powerful statement that we encounter all the time, and we have to understand that we are the owners of our minds and we have the power to be masters of how we think.

Our mindset is also shaped by our belief system. It is essential to develop the attitudes and values needed to fuel us in achieving something or failing to achieve something. In our daily tasks and any endeavour, the most important step is to have the right mindset. We need a mindset that whatever happens along the way in the course of implementing our plans, we will never succumb to the temptation of giving up. If we lose hope and give up, we can never reach our destination. If we have the right mindset, everything else will follow. It is tantamount to an analogy that mindset is an essential ingredient if we are preparing the best meal in our lifetime.

Navigating Common Mindsets of OFWs

Each of us is born with unique strengths, character and qualities. Considering that we have diverse origins, differing viewpoints, we also develop varying belief systems and frame of mind with different experiences and circumstances. But it is inherent within us to adapt and undergo transformation even in the way we think and the manner we establish our general outlook in life.

In the case of OFWs, we have different mindsets as we leave our country and find an opportunity in a foreign land. What, then, are the common mindsets and attitudes towards life among Filipino migrant workers? Coming from different backgrounds and circumstances, we have distinctive mindsets as we embark on our unique journey. Our mindset also contributes to shaping our habits, which are essential to achieving our goals.

Let us now navigate into common mindsets of Filipino migrant workers. These mindsets and attitudes, both positive and negative, may or may not be relatable to some Filipino migrant workers. There may be times when our mindset may not work to our favor in the beginning, but we need to nurture our mindset so that there is a paradigm shift in the way we set our direction towards attaining our ambitions.

- **Family First.** More often than not, OFWs are selfless. We think of our family first more than we think of our own needs. We are family-centred, willing to do whatever it takes for the sake of making a difference in our family. Every time our family needs help, we cannot afford to turn our backs on deaf ears. Depending on the gravity, we feel the urge to provide or extend some help. In most cases, family is always first, whether buying things or in troubling situations. Being situated miles away, it is natural to always worry or think about our families left behind. After all, it makes us happy to serve and provide for our families.

- **Sacrifice and Strong Determination.** Self-sacrifice is an innate character trait among many Filipinos. In the case of OFWs, being away from home is an emotional struggle in itself, considering we have already been soaked into several forms of trials in our everyday life abroad. But fulfilling our goals and enhancing our lives demands some sacrifices. More of us have hurdled extremely difficult situations in our home country, and that has made us stronger and more determined to keep going despite some hardships. And we develop the tenacity and unparalleled determination to overcome any obstacle that comes our way.

- **Cultural Adaptability.** Most Filipinos working abroad are very flexible and can readily adapt to the culture of the country in which they work. It is our natural way of blending into diverse cultures and following the rules and cultural norms of the country. For instance, in UAE, if you ask other nationalities about Filipinos, they would certainly perceive that we are easy to get along with and can adapt easily to the cultural setting of this country.

  We have that character of being lighthearted, easy to approach, and also the ability to learn fast about the rules and restrictions. We have high respect for other people and observe rules and regulations, especially when it comes to cultural practices and traditions. When we first enter into our workplace, we exercise prudence by asking about the culture and ethical practices of the company so as not to offend or cause undesirable acts.

- **Being Resilient.** Wherever we go and whatever harsh condition we are in, resilience culture has always been in our blood as Filipinos. From our home country we have already been subjected to many ups and downs in several aspects of our life. This made us resilient and tough and with what we have gone through, we don't allow ourselves to be defeated by inability to cope amidst the setbacks.

  Every time we encounter turning point and problems and we are swamped with unbearable pain, we don't just mourn, staring at nowhere. After some time, we compose ourselves and try to stand up, fighting to be alright and getting back on our feet to keep moving forward. We learn the lessons of our situation and try to maintain a strong fighting spirit to carry on with life, recover, and redeem ourselves.

- **Strong Community Support System.** The culture and mindset of "Bayanihan" can be observed among Filipinos anywhere in the world. Whenever we feel troubled and weary, we reach out to other Filipinos and other organizations for support. And the support system is always at hand knowing that there are still a lot of kind-hearted people ready to extend help to keep us going.

  There are many selfless people who are part of the community and have the mission to help others in need. Filipinos have various communities and groups convening regularly to propagate the spirit of kindness and volunteerism. Kindness is everywhere and, so we just need to reach out and admit that we need help. It is not embarrassing to ask for help, as long as you don't step on the rights of others. The community support system is a commonly practised habit, which is a positive trait that we bring with us wherever we are in the world.

- **Limiting Belief.** Sometimes, when we are relocated and out of our comfort zone, there is a tendency to think less of ourselves. We have the propensity to believe that we are not qualified, we're lagging behind and not competitive compared to other Filipinos or other nationalities. We set limitations in our minds, and we think in advance, and that preconceived idea is a limiting mindset. It is limiting in the sense that it is inimical to our plans and instead of nurturing our positive outlook, we end up being agitated by the thought that we will never succeed. If we try to assess and introspect, there is a limiting mindset, even from our point of origin and our upbringing. When we blend with others, we are ensnared by the belief that we still feel fragmented. But if there are gaps in our rearing, then we can work on and gradually practice the art of tuning into the right frame of mind.

- **Victim Mentality.** There is also some negative mindset existing among some OFWs that can affect the way we react to what happens to us at times. Sometimes, when there is an unfortunate incident or undesirable outcome, we don't take responsibility and admit our mistakes; instead, we blame others. We often claim to be victims, and it is not our own doing, making it an excuse not to rectify our deficiency, remedy the situation and institute the necessary changes in order to prevent the same incident in the future. If we let the victim mentality reside upon us, it will hamper our opportunity to grow because we don't acknowledge our flaws and imperfections.

- **Feeling Negative and Undervalued.** No matter how we set ourselves up to have a positive frame of mind, negative thoughts are inexorable. They come at any time and anywhere, especially when we feel alone with many uncertainties besieged in our minds. Sometimes, we feel undervalued and think that we cannot survive. The feeling of being negative is crippling and makes us think less of ourselves. We think we are inferior compared to others, and this is also connected to limiting belief. So, how do we feel undervalued in the context of being OFW? Some of us may think that we are always inferior and we have many insecurities. And to overcome this, we need to be our own energy booster. We need to be assertive and tell ourselves we are doing good and getting better to stop thinking that we are undervalued.

Making Decisions

How do you make decisions? Are you a fast decision-maker or someone who relies on other people's opinions? What is your mindset in making decisions?

Oftentimes, maybe we have experienced that our mind is trailing behind when we have choices to make in many aspects of our lives. It can be in a personal, career or any endeavour that requires informed decisions to make. In some cases, the choices are easily given to us, and we can decide quickly without apprehension or hesitation. However, there are times when we are in uncomfortable situations. For instance, when we need to decide on the choices at hand, it gives us more confusion than clarity. It can be likened to a hot seat where uncertainties can sometimes overpower the positive things about the options we have in mind. As the clock ticks, we feel the urgency, and that moment when we are more perplexed can sometimes be so discomforting.

Suppose you find an opportunity to join a new company and you need to decide to resign from your previous job, what would you do? What are the things you want to consider to make the right decision? I will relate my real experience in this aspect. When I joined my job, and the final stage of signing the contract took place, the personnel in charge of the overall hiring process handed me the contract requiring my signature. I saw other joiners who signed their contracts quickly, but it took me quite a long time to do the same. At first, the recruitment personnel explained and then asked me to read and affix my signature at the designated location. Certainly, it was a better opportunity, but I did not understand why it made me so uneasy, and I felt my mind was not giving me the go signal to sign it immediately. My heart was pounding faster, and after reading it twice, several thoughts of uncertainties and "what-ifs" were still flooding my mind.

When the HR personnel came for the second time to ask for a signed contract, I told him I needed some time to decide. He told me to take my time and read it again. I noticed new sets of joiners were coming, but I was still undecided. It was so confusing because earlier, it was clear that the benefits were way better in this company, but I seemed to have a "50-50" kind of thing in my mind, and I could not affix my signature. The HR personnel came for the third time and wondered why I still didn't sign it. He told me if I had not decided, I could bring the papers with the condition to protect its confidentiality and then come back when I finally signed it. I asked for his understanding and requested him to give me another chance to think deeply. At that time, I was sweating, and then I took a deep breath, I prayed for guidance, and then I called my husband. He told me to sign it without hesitation as it was my best option. To make the long story short, I affixed my signature and the recruitment personnel came for the fourth time, saying, "This is the first time I saw a Filipino having so much hesitation." I told him I was also wondering why I was in this situation, but I know this is the best career decision in my life.

Collaborating with Others

Are you a team player or a lone performer? Maybe in some situations, in personal or career, this may surface from time to time. There are some tasks that need to be completed faster when collaborating with others. There are times that require us to break free of the mentality that we need to be working alone and bear all the burden trying to prove that we are invincible. However, overconfidence can also endanger the outcome of some crucial tasks, and we need to reach out to other helping hands to bolster our capabilities and ensure that success can be attained.

We don't need to work in isolation. We need support and teamwork to complement good performance and augment our resources in order to bring about the best combination for excellence. When we encounter problems, collaboration is a great instrument to foster knowledge sharing to find the best solution, share resources and encourage creativity among team members in order to solve the problem. Collaboration is a good mindset that we need to develop as we journey through life.

Discipline and Perseverance

It is inherent in us that when we venture into something, we invest our time and efforts so we can implement better ways and strategies to achieve our goals. It requires a deep commitment to being consistent in our actions cascaded on a daily basis to establish good habits. Training our minds to be consistent and not give in to any distraction or temptation would require ample time to develop. The habit of maintaining discipline and perseverance is not an easy pursuit. We would be subjected to many twists and crossroads along the way, but we have to stay committed to persevere and never give up. This is a good quality for achieving success.

In hard times and catastrophe, our perseverance is also tested. Sometimes, it is easy to change plans and succumb to the temptation of giving up our dreams. By taking this route to mediocrity, we are made incapable of surpassing challenges. We need to train our minds to embrace the mindset of having that staying power to maintain our course until we reach our final destination. If we aspire to achieve something and make a difference, then we make adequate sacrifices that entail discipline in mind, body and spirit in order to persevere until success is at hand. It is not an easy journey, but we need interminable stamina fueled by discipline and perseverance.

Having a Good Learning Attitude

Our journey in life is not always smooth sailing. We are constantly confronted with many challenges, setbacks, ups and downs in the course of achieving our goals. Most of the time when we plunge, we devote more time blaming ourselves than standing up and learning from our mistakes.

If we fail to achieve the desired outcome, this means we still need time to learn and grow as there are lessons accorded upon us. We can learn new skills and enhance our capabilities, professionally, emotionally and spiritually, to stand against difficulties. Perhaps failure is an instrument to identify areas for improvement, and we can find ways to restructure our mindset. A good learning attitude is a positive frame of mind that we can institute to take that uphill battle of learning the hard way in order to fortify our potential. We can implore the attitude of admitting that life is a continual process of improving through the many lessons we learn as we journey towards achieving our goals.

Breaking Free from External Expectations

Are you a people-pleaser? What does it take to be yourself and break free from expectations? If we want to do good and have better performance just to please others, then we would end-up continually entangled in a virulent circus of pleasing other people and working towards their expectations. If we work for the glory of other people, we forget ourselves and then if we fail to please them, we would be disappointed, pressured and desperately anguished.

The fact that we focus on external expectations means that we tend to forget our own strategies and unique capabilities. We depend on other people's opinions instead of making internal fulfilment a key driver towards attaining stability in our actions as we work towards our goals. For example, as OFWs, sometimes we work for the expectations of other people not in the same situation as ours. This can be obstructive in our journey, as we already have a life laden with many obstacles. It is time to focus on our own and not get swayed by what people think and expect from us. We have the power to break free from this mental toxicity and move forward with the right mindset fastened with the right purpose.

Embracing Change in Mindset

Considering we have delved deeper and unveiled different mindsets and attitudes - both positive and negative, we can influence our thinking to change and transform into better versions of ourselves. How can we change our mindset or how can we facilitate change of mindset to take place?

We can always develop ways to have that paradigm shift and embrace a change in mindset. Let me tell you some general tips. I have implemented some of these in my own life.

- We have to undertake self-reflection and evaluate ourselves to determine our frame of mind and outlook on life.

- We have to acknowledge that we need some improvement in the way we think, our perceptions towards others, and the way we deal with essential matters in life.

- Challenge ourselves to minimize negative thoughts and instead just let them pass in fleeting moments and then focus on the many positive things in our life.

- Surround yourself with like-minded and positive people to absorb positive energy and feel reinvigorated.

- Be grateful and always think about where you came from and the people who helped you, and implore the art of never-ending gratitude.

- Learn from mistakes and have an open mind for feedback.

- Embrace the idea that we are continually growing and moving forward in a productive way.

- Invoke the power of divine intervention and have sustained faith that our life will get better and that we deserve abundance, not scarcity.

CHAPTER 4

MANAGING YOUR EMOTIONS

Life is full of trials and there's no escaping from its emotional turbulence. When we experience internal chaos, we often ask ourselves if we can survive. It takes a lot of strength, courage and determination to be able to weather all sorts of difficulties. And when psychological crises arise, it is all the more intractable to carry on. In all facets of life, we are engulfed with different emotions. Are we emotionally prepared?

When we are subjected to challenging times, it is overwhelming, and sometimes we lose our focus, and this needs a structured approach in terms of finding solutions. There may be times we feel unlucky, but we cannot predict any outcome and this entails emotional struggle as to how we accept the things happening at hand. And to manage the complexities of our emotions, we have to nurture emotional intelligence.

What is Emotional Intelligence? Why is it Important?

According to Oxford Learner's Dictionaries, Emotional Intelligence (EI) is the ability to understand your emotions and those of other people and to behave appropriately in different situations (https://www.oxfordlearnersdictionaries.com/). It covers a wide range of skills and competencies in dealing with the emotional aspects of humans, managing and confronting our own feelings and others with whom we interact. In our everyday lives, we are engulfed with different emotions and the spectacle that comes with every emotion we display. EI is essential in the overall development and well-being in terms of handling social and relationship aspects as we encounter different personalities in our lives.

There are many areas encompassing the development of EI, but let us try to delve on the practical application in our daily life. And in many areas of our life, if we can effectively manage our emotions, then we can maintain the right balance as to how to respond to specific situations that call for prudence in the way we think, say and act.

In the context of OFWs, where life is much more challenging and exposed to massive concerns with different drawbacks, nurturing EI is an essential ingredient in order to cope in upsetting circumstances. We have to develop skill sets that can intensify our personal and professional capabilities as we aspire to attain success. The challenge is how we can be able to consistently improve and acquire constructive feedback that serves as building blocks as we become battle-hardened in terms of emotional struggles as migrant workers.

Identifying and Understanding Your Emotions

Have you encountered some horrible situations in your life that made you feel confused, not knowing how to react and feel for a certain moment? Perhaps some of us may have some incidents that make us wonder why we respond or react that way. After reflecting on it, we realize that we could have reacted the other way around. Sometimes, we don't know our feelings and we don't know how to react appropriately. In this case, we need to identify our emotions first since we don't know how to nurture the right way to deal with them if, in the first place, we are not even sure of our feelings. The way we feel and express ourselves is very important. It is as good as saying that we don't know where to go if we don't know where to start.

Identifying and understanding our emotions entails a structured approach and constant self-evaluation using some tools and techniques that we can harness through experience and some generally practised ways. There is no standard equation to identify and understand our emotions. These may include self-reflection to assess ourselves, writing down our feelings at a particular point in time, reflecting on past experiences, being mindful of how we feel and how we react, assessing our physical sensation when we feel something, and learning techniques from reading or even free videos. Whatever technique that works in our favor can be helpful. It is not an overnight success, it needs time to develop.

As human beings, our emotions are complex and multifaceted. If we are bewildered at times and don't understand our emotions, it is totally alright. The skills of understanding can be acquired through time if we are consistent to go through the continual process of reflection and exploring other techniques mirroring our inner experiences. Eventually, we can develop self-awareness and slowly understand our emotions. If we have that incessant desire to navigate the journey of effectively managing our emotions, then we are working towards making ourselves better.

Expressing Emotions Effectively

As human beings, we have frailties and we are not always masters of our own emotions. We have many lapses, misgivings and frustrations. Every time we deal with people, the way we feel towards something may not be expressed in the right perspective. For example, if we are upset or disappointed, we sometimes forget how to control our emotions and utter words that can hurt people's feelings. There are times that instead of being constructive, we find fault in others to make ourselves righteous. We resort to blame games without acknowledging that we, too, are part of the distasteful outcome.

The right expression of emotion is essential in our interaction with people, be it personal, career or family life. If we lose control of what we say, then the consequences can sometimes be disheartening. We cannot undo the words we utter. Expressing our emotions effectively requires constant self-evaluation and self-reflection to check ourselves and see if we have the right manner of expressing them to others. It is key to understand yourself, understand others and understand the overall situation as a whole.

If we have identified our emotions properly, then they have to be expressed correctly. When we display our emotions, we have to be consciously reminded that we deal with human beings and that they have their own feelings, too. We can develop the ability to choose the right words and express them in a respectful manner. We have to be honest, authentic and genuine. Feelings cannot be faked most of the time; they can be seen by others, and the way we express them can have either beneficial or detrimental impacts on other people. If there are problems, we have to be specific to that particular problem and not bring back issues in the past. Admitting our shortcomings can give us a constructive avenue to indemnify spiteful actions.

Another constructive expression of emotions is showing empathy instead of trying to pin people down. It is worthwhile to put yourself in other people's shoes and try to reflect on how it feels if you are in their situation. There are people around who seem to be insensitive to the ordeal we're going through. Instead of showing empathy, they are in a celebratory mood and wallow amidst our misery. It is better to offer a solution than trying to worsen the problem. Several ways may work for some, while others may have different experiences. But more importantly, we have to be mindful every time we express our emotions in any situation.

Overcoming Fears

What is your greatest fear in life? Each of us has its own fear. Generally, there can be a multitude of fears – fear of heights, fear of darkness, fear of the unknown, fear of death, fear of speaking in public, fear of failure, fear to try and many others. What is fear? And how can we conquer it? According to the APA Dictionary of Psychology (https://dictionary.apa.org/fear), fear is "a basic, intense emotion aroused by the detection of imminent threat, involving an immediate alarm reaction that mobilizes the organism by triggering a set of physiological changes." Fear can be a limiting factor that is difficult to conquer if we are dominated by the negative emotions brought about by having a terrible feeling. We can have anxiety confronting our fears, and most of the time, we cannot understand how we respond to any situation we dread about. Fear may be connected to our past or something to do with our future. We feel we are strained to try something because, in our mind, we already foresee that this thing will happen even if it is far from reality.

Fears can come in many forms, and we can navigate through them by identifying them in the first place. Let us take some examples of common fears in the context of being Filipino migrant workers. Being a migrant worker myself, I share some of these fears and they may or may not be relatable to others. Our fears include fear of failure, fear of loss in many aspects of our personal and career lives, and fear of being judged by others that we would not improve our lives despite being migrant workers for a considerable period of time. In many ways, we need to identify what we fear about, challenge ourselves to obliterate negative thoughts and embrace positivity and optimism.

We don't need to be fearless, but we have to face and confront our fears with courage. If fear is limiting us to exert effort, then all the more that we have to push ourselves to conquer our fears. It requires gradual changes, in tiny steps, to slowly break from the bondage of that fear in our mind. We need to convince ourselves by reflecting and taking that inner drive to muster the unyielding courage to overcome our fears. As we are confronted with fears, we have to have the valor to face them and not perpetually evade them. As Nelson Mandela says, "The brave man is not he who does not feel afraid, but he who conquers that fear."

Coping With Grief

For as long as we breathe, grief is inevitable. It has been part and parcel of being human as we journey through life. Striking unexpectedly, grief leaves our hearts with scars that take time and enormous energy to heal. These indelible marks on our hearts can be devastating. Grief is painful. Excruciatingly painful.

What are the things that we grieve about? Grief comes in many unimaginable forms. We can't always know beforehand how we would live with it and embrace it. It strikes unexpectedly, leaving us unprepared to deal with it. For example, in our love life, the loss of a loved one, losing a job, distress from day-to-day misgivings and failures—grief shows up in several aspects of our lives. Differing from person to person, the gravity of how grief impacts us depends on how deeply we are associated with the object of our sadness.

As grief strikes in different ways, it is processed in several different forms as well. According to a commonly cited reference in her book "On Death and Dying", published in 1969, Elisabeth Kübler-Ross discussed five stages of grief. This has been widely referenced in some research, too, and I have taken it verbatim as cited in a study, "Grieving and Death." The five stages of grief she defined are as follows:

Denial: Rejection or refusal to accept the truth. This is also known as shock.

Anger: Physical expressions of hostility directed towards people and God.

Bargaining: An agreement between the conscious mind and soul involving a negotiation for more time to live.

Depression: Reactive grief over a specific loss and preparatory loss over their coming death.

Acceptance: An acceptance of existing conditions and receptivity to things that can't be changed.

How do we cope with grief? No matter how emotionally crushed and deeply broken we feel, we always find ways to survive and confront our grief. As everybody deals with grief uniquely, no universal or perfect formula exists. As we move through grief at our own unique pace, we set out to restore our physical, emotional, mental, and overall well-being.

As I have experienced deeper desolation in grief while being away, I list down some practical ways to cope with it. You may see if it seems relatable to you, too.

- Seeking divine intervention and providence through profound praying and reflection.

- Strong support system from family, friends and colleagues.

- Embrace your sorrow and just mourn.

- Temporarily cutting off communication with others except family.

- Taking a hiatus from online interaction and deactivating social media accounts for a period of time.

- Reading and writing to alleviate stress.

- Learning new skills for pastimes.

We constantly explore a variety of coping strategies and survival mechanisms in an attempt to liberate some of the pain. Some ways work for others, while some don't, and in the end, we adopt what is tailored to our emotional needs with the end goal of alleviating our distress and seeing some light at the end of the tunnel. With grief, we hope to widen our grasp of life's several complexities.

In grief, we can also embrace some lessons from our own experience and the way we cope up. Let's take, for example, my personal journey when I lost my father as an OFW; grief taught me a lot. With his demise, I was crushed, mourned deeply and heavily devastated. But it has also toughened me with resilience and showed me how I could weather anything as long as I was committed to reflecting on all that happened by looking beyond the grief itself.

With grief, I learned that no sad times must annihilate my dreams and hopes to be a better person, and the sooner I decide to flush sorrow out of my system, the better. Healing is an end result, but not the centrepiece—I need to benefit with every small step I take towards moving forward. We get to internalize the lessons from our sorrows and use them as guiding principles for the rest of our lives.

Although broken and shattered in our grief, we need not stay that way forever. We need to move forward and pick up the fragments of our wounded heart. Our pain and new lessons can fuel our progress and equip us better as we move through more disasters in our lives. In the end, an essential ingredient to seeking the strength to power through is seeking divine intervention and providence to relieve us of our pain and desolation so we can move ahead with the healing process and get through life with our greater purpose.

Managing Anger

At some point in our lives, there are times that we get out of control when we're extremely indignant. We lose control over the situation when we're driven by that feeling of exasperation. Sometimes, we express it by venting out unpalatable words that can hurt the feelings of other people around us. Did you ever feel extremely angry? What would you do if you were in this situation? Being upset is normal for a human being. However, feeling discomfort out of anger can happen in any situation, whether personal, family, career, or any minor issue in daily life. Getting angry is inevitable as long as we are alive and interacting with people because anything can happen at any time in our dealings, relationships and events.

But staying upset and letting the anger topple down our emotional stability for a longer period of time can be damaging to our health and overall well-being while inflicting hurt on other people, causing strain to harmonious relationships. We need to hone our skills in taking control of our emotions and expressing our anger. There are many instances where anger can be a trigger for us to succumb to emotional chaos since we lose control and anger dominates our feelings. Some examples that can make us extremely upset include situations where we don't get the desired outcome, when someone utters provocative words, when someone crosses the line, or when someone behaves rudely and arrogantly. There are many infuriating situations that cause us to backfire with uncontrollable vindictive behaviour, and that can result in cursing and resentful actions.

When we let rage be the predominant thought in our minds, then we become subservient to this feeling, which ends up manifesting in our actions. Some people may even take revenge on the wrong people and wrong situations since they cannot control their anger. There are times that we resort to countering it with equally hurtful defences on an uncontrollable scale. No matter how we try to control ourselves, we go beyond equitable response. This necessitates us to employ conscious evaluation of how we think and how we feel internally and utilize our power to take control. Managing our anger is an essential skill in maintaining harmonious relationships with individuals around us.

There are many practical ways of managing our anger. We can be mindful and hone our skills in harnessing self-awareness and self-restraint and practice prudence to alleviate the outrage. The ability to take respite and become insightful is necessary in the face of anger. Sometimes, it requires us to sanitize our language.

We need to think many times before venting out so we can choose what to say and when to say the right words. One strategy is to reflect and put ourselves in the situation of others at the receiving end and then try to discern how it feels like. By trying to put ourselves in other peoples' shoes, only then can we realize that we need to be prudent and cautious of how it can be injurious when things get out of control.

The adverse impact of venting out anger on an uncontrollable scale can jeopardize our goal of maintaining balance in every situation. It may cause damage to people physically, emotionally, and psychologically and even cause damage to property. That's why we have to gain the necessary skills to control our anger. And through time and constant reflection, by being mindful, we can slowly become the master of controlling it and not the other way around. Let it start with internal reflection and moving tiny steps to enhance our capability in managing our anger. As Bruce Lee said, "Emotion can be the enemy, if you give into your emotion, you lose yourself. You must be at one with your emotions because the body always follows the mind."

Overcoming Homesickness and Depression

One specific example of being overwhelmed with homesickness is the life of a migrant worker. Being away from home is an emotional struggle in itself. Of the several things you have to cope with, homesickness gets the largest piece of the pie. Personally, living as an expatriate in Dubai took me a while to realign and feel emotionally settled. The struggles were real, but fulfilling my goals required sacrifices. Our journey is already ingrained with vulnerability to homesickness and complexity that brings with it disdain.

The anxiety of keeping the physical distance can be enormous. There are many instances and events where we feel nostalgic. As much as we would evade being melodramatic, as you're away for a long time, you find yourself wishing for your homeland to be just a fence away—you could simply jump over and reunite with your family and find fleeting solace amidst extreme loneliness. But sometimes, we traverse through dreams and desires and yearn to let our senses slumber as we float through a soothing wonderland born out of our wishful thinking. Despite this despondent feeling of homesickness, we have a mission to fulfil, and we should not succumb to depression.

There are many ways to cope with homesickness and depressing situations while in a foreign land. We have chosen this path of the "road less travelled by", as they say, and so we have to muster the emotional strength and ability to win over homesickness. We can indulge in worthwhile activities to pass the time and engage with people with the same interests to alleviate our emotional struggles. Having effective communication and staying connected with our family and loved ones are crucial elements in mitigating homesickness. While being away, we can focus on our work while enjoying the pastime, hobbies and many other activities to deviate attention away from loneliness. For instance, we can devote adequate time to praying and meditation, engaging in sports, daily routine and exercise, reading, writing, honing our skills in cooking, doing volunteer work, watching inspirational videos, karaoke sessions, and many other things that are beneficial to our well-being.

It is truly self-sacrifice, but we have chosen to be away, and instead of feeling depressed, we just need to be positive and do worthwhile things to cope with homesickness. Instead of blaming ourselves, think of the bigger picture that what we're doing is for the greater good of our families and to have a happy and fulfilled life.

Motivating Yourself and Motivating Others

In our daily life, we often experience bad days. With the many trials and hardships, our fragmented emotions need a heap of motivation and positive undertakings to divert ourselves from the weakening impact of desolation. Sometimes, we lack motivation, feel sluggish and need that energy to kick-start. If we cannot motivate ourselves, we certainly cannot be a source of motivation for other people around us.

So, how can we fight demotivation and muster the courage to get moving? It starts from deep within, knowing ourselves better and connecting to our purpose can be a guiding star to motivate ourselves. And when we are motivated, we radiate that drive to inspire other people as well. There are many techniques we can explore in terms of self-motivation. Simple routines such as counting our blessings and thinking positively starting from the moment we wake up in the morning can be a powerful tool to foster the power of self-motivation. It gives us the drive and burning desire to be productive and maintain the energy towards achieving our goals in life.

For instance, as migrant workers, we can reflect on our deep purpose and why we work in a foreign land. That drive to fulfil our ambition necessitates us to be strong and continue even if we are struggling, giving ourselves that consciousness that no matter what happens, we will never give up. In times of desperation, we continually try to push ourselves and, in the process, try to encourage others never to lose hope. We don't need a giant leap, we just need to get up and wipe off the impediment in our mind to take the first step. If we are motivated, then we create a positive emotional environment for others in terms of personal and professional growth.

If we can only radiate positive energy and motivate others, it will uplift some of those who have full of self-doubt and lost the will to carry on. Let me share my real experience of propelling motivation in a writing boot camp, despite the fact that I was also on the verge of losing my way as a writer. At that time, I was also struggling with some issues.

To encapsulate in few words, I told them that I was once like them, full of limiting beliefs and fears. But I conquered my fears, followed professional advices from my coach and just continue to write every day even when I don't feel like writing and I have writer's block. I continued to inspire them by saying, "don't underestimate yourself, take responsibility and believe that you can do it. Don't doubt your abilities and believe that you are already Authors. I once dreamed of writing my own book, and I followed that dream. Let us journey together as authors."

In the end, even if we are facing storms in life, we can still motivate others. And if we can be a source of a little inspiration for others, then it feels fulfilling.

CHAPTER 5

DEALING WITH STRESS

"It is not the events of our lives that shape us,

but our beliefs as to what those events mean."

~ Tony Robbins

In our everyday lives, we encounter many stressors. It is not always plain sailing, and we are subjected to challenging situations in many aspects of our lives. We can have stress in our midst at any time. But if we let our emotions be dominated by how stressful a certain situation is, then we may end up losing the grip to connect to our purpose and be consumed by negativity. How do we respond to a stressful situation? We cannot escape stress, and we need a deeper understanding of how we can combat stress.

Understanding Stress

What is stress? According to the World Health Organization (WHO), "Stress can be defined as a state of worry or mental tension caused by a difficult situation. Stress is a natural human response that prompts us to address challenges and threats in our lives. Everyone experiences stress to some degree. The way we respond to stress, however, makes a big difference to our overall well-being." (https://www.who.int//news-room/questions-and-answers/item/stress/)

Stress can manifest in many ways. In our daily hustles in life, we are exposed to many situations that can be a stressor, from minor or negligible things to bigger and more important issues in life. When we feel uncomfortable, we cannot hide it from our facial expressions, and it can affect how we conduct ourselves during the course of our interaction with other people. It can be issues in our home, our family, anxieties from separation or distance, work-related and many insuperable forms of stressors. Let us explore why we are stressed and what the common causes of stress are. If we understand and know where it is coming from, then we can nurture ourselves to find ways and means to combat stress or find an antidote to stress. Like many other infelicitous feelings, stress can be detrimental to our health.

Why are we stressed, and what are the usual causes of stress? Stress can be at varying levels and it strikes us in different ways. We can be vulnerable to different causes of stress. There is stress coming from minor issues in our family, relationships, petty issues, stress from work, financial stress, health concerns, mental anguish and many other things that come our way that we keep overthinking. Some can be from recurring issues, while some may come from unexpected incidents that can trigger mood swings and cause stress in a short period of time. Or maybe some may have experienced stress from being unable to sleep due to guilty feelings or bothered conscience.

No matter how stressful the situation is, we can always choose and control how we respond and react. The way we control our thoughts is very important in dealing with stress. We can always alleviate the distressing situation by starting from our mindset. When we overthink any situation beyond our control, then we succumb to a stress level that can later escalate if we try to harbour it inside. If we submerge ourselves into emotional or physical stress, it can weaken our system and the negative energy will keep us unable to do anything productive.

Common Stress Among OFWs

As Filipino migrant workers, we are already faced with many challenging situations. What is the usual stress of OFWs? Let us look through some of the common stress, which may be true or relatable to some, depending on their situations.

- **Stress from Homesickness.** Leaving our families behind is daunting, and every time we think of them, we are inevitably stressed out. If we keep on overthinking, the situation can be tormenting. Sometimes, we have that dominant thought that if only not for a bigger purpose, then we would not venture into a foreign land. It is sometimes unfathomable how we miss some important milestones and occasions of our loved ones, but we have decided to take this route and so we continually find ways to alleviate the sadness brought about by homesickness.

- **Financial Pressure.** Issues pertaining to finances can also be a common stress factor among migrant workers. Some situations include inability to meet financial demands of family back home, overspending and unable to have savings from monthly income, pressure coming from debts, financial deficit from compulsive shopping, and many other issues revolving around money matters. We may also experience deception and be doomed to financial loss because of betrayal and unjustified vengeful acts.

- **Health Issues.** Stress also comes in the form of chronic and life-threatening illnesses like cancer. Health issues can be difficult to process and feel like a terrifying nightmare, especially when you sense the face of death getting closer. The distress isn't only limited to you but also extends to your family and loved ones as they need time to take in the uncertainty that revolves around the rest of your life. The fact that your precious life could perish at any moment takes a while to sink in. People close to us may often be in denial and it implies escalating pain as you approach acceptance and total surrender to the Creator with the realization that everyone must embrace mortality.

Being a migrant worker, times like these can easily make you feel like you've hit rock bottom and the sense of complete devastation leaves you feeling lost—taking a single step further or starting somewhere seems impossible.

Several what-ifs and doubts start clouding your mind.

Will I be able to survive this?

How will I get through this?

How much time do I have left?

And although your nears and dears are often dependent on you, the thought of leaving them all behind makes you crave for their soothing embrace to neutralize the sorrow you feel. But these wishful delusions feel hopeless with them being far, far away. It feels like when a superstorm hits—you don't know how to regain your strength and how to reinstate your sanity for survival mode to kick in.

As an example, I had my share of COVID-19 experience, but my battle with the virus was more on the mental or psychological side rather than on the physical side, given the asymptomatic nature. The stress was enormously overwhelming and home isolation meant that I had to be alone with no interaction with the outside world. It was quite excruciating, I had to muster up some inner strength to detach from the fear to stop overthinking about all that could go wrong while I lived in a foreign land. I longed for the day to be freed of it all as I dealt with the psychological monstrosities building up inside.

- **Stress on Relationships and Conflicts.** Another commonly experienced type of stress is matters of the heart, like break-ups in relationships, conflicts with family or friends. The reasons could be several—irreconcilable differences, major fights, being unable to patch things up in some situations. Sad episodes like these may leave us feeling melodramatic and crushed within, and our broken hearts need some time and energy to heal. Acceptance and moving on can feel quite daunting.

- **Work-related Stress.** We can also be exposed to several stresses at our workplace, considering that we need more time to adjust to the new work environment, new company culture, and many other things in our careers. Sometimes, in our workplace, we tend to overstress with minor issues that cloud our minds because of apprehensions, fear, and lack of self-confidence. During unfortunate events, where we can lose our jobs, it is also a major cause of stress, taking into account that we have to provide for our family's sustenance.

- **Loss of Family and Loved Ones.** As humans, we are fragile and vulnerable to anything unwanted that comes our way. We are seldom prepared to deal with the stress and devastation that the loss of a loved one may bring. Given our close association with the departed, the pain of them being gone from this existence feels agonizing. They could be anybody—immediate family, close friends, relatives, someone who profoundly impacted our life. Extreme loneliness, isolation and depression are some of the manifestations that approach us in the face of saddening conditions that need to be processed from the inside out. Differing from person to person, the gravity of how losing a loved one and family members impacts us depends on how deeply we are associated with them.

Practical Ways for Relieving Stress

Having known that we are experiencing stress in our daily lives, we cannot allow ourselves to be consumed by this negative emotion and become unproductive. We need to deal with it, confront it head on and try to find practical ways to win over it. It may be an uphill battle, but the most important thing is that we have to be optimistic and be our own staunch ally to drive away distress.

As we are deeply wounded and in despair, we need strength to carry on. It may not be true to all, but more often, we feel isolated and are deeply engrossed with negative thoughts rather than embracing positive ones. With strong will and grit, we can divert our attention and engage in other activities for a positive outcome.

There is no magic potion in dealing with stress. Each of us has its own strategy that serves the purpose well in relieving stress. Stress is a health concern that can be experienced by people from all walks of life, in any profession or status in life. Let us explore some ways to de-stress, unveiling some examples which may or may not be relatable to others. I have personally tried many of these practical ways:

- **Praying or Meditation.** Seeking divine guidance through reflections in prayers is a powerful tool to ease anxiety and worries. Some people may use meditation techniques that can be learned from some practising experts. When we pray or reflect in silence, this gives us a chance to evaluate how we feel from deep within while seeking divine intervention. In solitude, we can talk to God, talk to our inner self, free our minds from negativities and release stress. Praying can be anywhere and anytime, as long as you acknowledge the presence of the Divine power. We can also join some scheduled prayer times and other activities to enhance our spiritual well-being.

- **Reading and Writing to Alleviate Stress.** Reading books is a good diversion when we are stress-out. Reading can enhance our comprehension, teaching us new things and a good way to relax or momentarily detach from anxiety. It can make us navigate through different places and situations that we can enjoy from the books we read.

Along the same lines, writing is also a worthwhile activity to leave distress and pain on the sidetrack. For instance, I am not a gregarious person, and I have used writing to express my thoughts and vent out my emotions. Writing isn't limited to writing a book or something to be published; it is simply penning down your thoughts, which weigh heavily in your emotional baggage. Writing how you feel when loneliness consumes you and seeing it on a piece of paper will offer you some amount of comfort. Unleashing your emotions helps you to cleanse your mind and leaves you feeling better. It will also clear your mind and create space for rational thinking rather than staying emotionally down most of the time.

- **Watching Funny Videos.** Nowadays, online videos can be accessible anytime. Watching funny videos can make us laugh and make us forget our problems momentarily. When we laugh, it ignites the drive to be happy, thereby creating more space for blissfulness. One rich platform to access funny videos is YouTube, and we can do it while resting. We know for sure that if there's something funny, we are triggered to indulge in it and start laughing. It is contagious, so other people around us may also share the laughter.

- **Listening to Music.** Mostly, when we listen to our favourite song, it can stimulate a feeling of relief, and we can relax while reconnecting to good memories. At times, it can also be emotional and melodramatic, but the emotions unravelled can lead to relieving our stress. Music diverts our attention from overthinking a troubling situation at hand. Good music, whether you're alone or with good company, can be very calming and therapeutic.

- **Hobby and Pastime.** In order to de-stress, we can also indulge in something as a pastime or join some groups that promote our hobby. It can be sports activities, cooking, painting or any other worthwhile activities that may enhance our skills while releasing stress.

- **Healthy Lifestyle.** Eating healthy food is essential in proper nourishment of our body. If we have a healthier body, we can also have a healthier mind. Having a good sleep is also very important. Proper nutrition and adequate sleep along with some exercise can be a good way to re-energize ourselves and get rid of stress.

- **Walking or Connecting With Nature.** A simple routine of walking in the park or connecting with nature is a good stress reliever. Walking is a good way to relieve stress since you will change your environment and breathe fresh air, in addition to losing some calories for a healthier body. It is nurturing your connection with the natural environment and keeping the consciousness that, as human beings, we need to recharge once in a while.

- **Connect to Important People.** If we are stressed, we can talk it out with our family, spouse, partner, best friend or any trusted life advisor through a good communication strategy. By reaching out and talking, we can find an avenue for kindness and empathy from those who truly care for us. In this manner, we would find some comfort in knowing that we are not alone in our troubles and heartbreaking moments. For example, if you connect with a trusted friend who is in the same predicament as yours, you somehow share the burden and it will be a relief because of someone's genuine care and concern. We can also connect with support communities that have welfare programs for the distressed. And the community can be an avenue where we can undergo counselling or become productive through charitable works.

- **Simple Get-away.** In order to break the monotony of our everyday routine and some stressors, we can have a simple getaway, exploring places to unwind and have fun while releasing stress. For example, a visit to a nearby beach or tourist attraction with family or friends can weather away some tension, gradually eliminating the adverse impact of some difficult situations. Life is still beautiful to enjoy in simple ways and not to be soaked with problems and devastations, but to promote mental and emotional relaxation.

Managing Workplace Stress

As working individuals, we know that our workplace is an important part of our system. Sometimes, we consider it as our second home. It is where we are nurtured and developed as productive and responsible professionals. However, we are also exposed to different stressful situations at work. For example, if we feel we are not treated fairly by our colleagues or superiors, then we can feel devastated and aloof. Depending on our roles and responsibilities, our work can also be a source of stress, especially when meeting deadlines for assigned tasks. We can also be stressed by our insecurities at work or some feelings of being undervalued. Sometimes, our predominant thoughts on untoward events or miscommunication may cause some negative emotions.

So, how can we manage stress at work? Let us explore some strategies that offer a meaningful and constructive way to alleviate stress in day-to-day life in our workplace. In any workplace, stress is normal and it is up to us to carry ourselves to tackle issues in such a way that we surpass difficult situations and focus on our responsibilities to perform our job well and work harmoniously with our colleagues. There are situations that call for our professional prudence and adjustment is necessary as people come from diverse backgrounds.

When there is a stressful situation at work, don't let it destroy and bother you, instead always think positive and propagate optimism. Always have time to smile and take things lightly with the thought that the situation will eventually get better. If someone is offending us or throwing some hurtful remarks, we don't need to fight back and stoop down to their level. We need to be cautious and act with utmost professionalism. If we try to focus on ourselves, we don't have time to compare ourselves with others. We have to avoid undignified comparison and stereotyping because it can lead to unhappy and negative thoughts.

When someone spreads negative thoughts, be the positive ambassador and counter it with the good things about the situation. Reflect on the good things you have been blessed with from your work. Work is a gift and we should nurture gratitude and always look at the positive side of every situation. We need to remind ourselves that we are here to work and perform to the best of our abilities. We don't focus on situations which can make us miserable. Instead, we need to shift our focus on the positive things and look for opportunities to grow or progress in our careers.

Work stress can be better managed with patience, good communication and excellent performance. For example, we should learn to prioritize our tasks according to urgency and importance so that we would not be stressed out with beating deadlines without compromising the quality of work. Understanding our colleagues and situations is necessary. We should have a positive mindset at work that for every challenging situation, there is always a solution to make things better. Effectively overcoming stress at work and maintaining a positive work environment can be instrumental to achieving our goals and cultivating a culture of excellence.

Being Happy With Yourself

The best way to combat stress is to think of happy moments and just be happy with ourselves. Being joyful means we feel secure and content with what we have and not jealous of what other people have. If we are happy, that means we are optimistic and we always look at the positive side of any circumstance. Happy people are those who enjoy life even in simple pleasures on a day-to-day basis. Happiness emanates from deep within. If we are silent and calm, it doesn't mean that we are unhappy. Happiness is a feeling of being content with who we are and without feeling envious of others.

Believing in our own skills and abilities can drive away insecurities and limiting beliefs. Each of us is born unique with a unique set of talents. Every time we feel that emptiness inside, we have the sole responsibility to ignite our own positive emotions. Positivity and exuberance replace that emptiness with a happy disposition and contentment. Happiness and contentment are states of mind, and when we fill our minds with happy thoughts, we feel empowered and good about ourselves.

We don't need validation and praise from people around us to be happy and content, we just need to start from our mindset. Let us have a happy and contented frame of mind, and our positive outlook in life can bring about happiness from deep within. Our happiness will radiate and transcend through endless possibilities in making other people happy as well. So, we have to work from our inner selves and slowly get rid of stress to have a happy and fulfilled life.

ENHANCING FINANCIAL LITERACY

Time and again, we could experience financial woes. We encounter problems with money matters and how we manage our finances, resulting in our inability to sustain a good life. If we lack financial literacy, then we cannot have a bigger picture to weather the challenges and still fulfil our goal of having financial freedom. Our ability and skills to handle our money can be acquired through years of experience. If we are keen to learn and educate ourselves, then we can avoid pitfalls that can hamper our way to achieving financial goals and living the abundant life we deserve.

Financial Management is Important

Proper management is very important in any aspect of our life. If we don't know how to manage things well, then we can experience a lot of problems when things go crazy and seemingly uncontrollable. When it comes to our finances, management is of utmost importance. We need money for our sustenance, and we have to allocate our income well because it is hard-earned money.

Financial management is a subject where most of us need to enhance our literacy level. As working individuals, sometimes we cannot figure out how to budget our income properly, how to spend wisely and how to save money despite our meagre income from our job. In the case of people working abroad, for OFWs specifically, we have our unique timeline and journey in our employment. It is important that we set our goals and implement strategies in order to reach our goals at some point in time. Of course, it is undeniable that we can commit mistakes, make wrong decisions, and misdirect our actions, all of which can lead to financial problems. But we need to bounce back and check our personal finances, then try to evaluate what went wrong to rectify the root cause of the problem.

In managing our finances, we need to know where we are, so that we can address our shortcomings and we know where we are heading to. If we don't know where we stand, then we might end up regretting in the end on being remiss with the opportunities bestowed upon us. There are many generally prescribed ways to enhance our financial literacy, but our mindset is very important. Our thoughts are vital in guiding us and setting our perspective about money and how to utilize it wisely on essential things.

Setting Priorities

We cannot escape from any mess. We are subjected to many challenging situations in our daily lives. Nonetheless, we can set our priorities well so that we do not go astray and stay on track with our financial goals. In the aspect of financial management, setting priorities is of paramount concern. If we don't know our priorities, then we may spend lavishly on non-essential things, and we end up choked with stress on our finances.

So when we earn money, what comes first in our mind? Before we spend it on other things, we have to connect it to our priorities in life. Many, if not all, will agree that family is our top priority. We think of our families first before our own needs, and we are always ready to sacrifice to put their needs before our own. In the first place, our families are our inspiration, and they are the reason why we have the energy to start our mornings.

For OFWs, our families are the reasons why we pursue opportunities in foreign lands. We always look after the basic needs of our immediate family and try to squeeze our budget to make ends meet. The common phrase "family first" echoes in every one of us and it resonates with deeper meaning and purpose. And because of our families, we are willing to do everything for them. When there are times that we become weary and unmotivated, we just need to reflect and think of our families to regain that drive and keep moving ahead to reach our goals.

Learning How to Save

Undeniably, we are always confronted with different issues concerning our finances. We may have decent income to support our needs, but when an emergency comes, we can be heavily burdened and it can cause worries especially in unexpected situations. If we run short of budget, we usually turn to family and friends for a rescue whenever possible. Or in the worst case scenario, we don't have a choice but to avail bank loans just to provide for our urgent needs.

As we are vulnerable to different financial challenges, it is necessary for us to save money from our income. 'Saving for the rainy days', as they say, so that we can have a spare in case we have to spend on something urgent. It will also spare us from the pressure of additional payment or deduction from our monthly income. Saving is a good habit to develop, and if we know how to save appropriately, we will be able to stay on track with our long-term financial goals. What are our priorities in terms of saving? Let us go through some specific examples from a migrant worker's perspective. This can also be used by anyone who is keen to save money towards a better future.

- **Setting up an Emergency Fund.** More often than not, emergency situations come unexpectedly. Instead of being stressed out looking for someone to lend some money, we can set up an emergency fund from our income. Even if we start with a smaller amount, at least we can be ready and will have some funds in times of difficulty. This can also be something to utilize for giving assistance or helping a family in dire need.

- **Saving for Education.** One important aspect of looking after the future of our families is saving for the educational expenses of our children. For example, if we are earning from our salary and our child is still in pre-school or elementary days, we can establish a plan to allocate regular savings intended for her/his college education after several years. As we know, college education would take the biggest chunk of the educational expenses. Saving ahead, while we are able, is the key to a well-established educational fund for the future of our children.

• **Saving for Retirement.** On the other hand, while helping our families in times of dire need and saving for our children, we also need to think of ourselves. In the context of being a migrant worker, after some time, when we reach our target, we need to be back home. Depending on our individual journey, most of us will have some retirement plans as to what we will be doing for the rest of our lives after our stint as OFWs. But we cannot work all the time; we have our limitations. We deserve to have something for ourselves and our future expenses, which include health-related expenses, sustenance and overall well-being.

Living a Simple Life

If you had to choose a way of living, would you opt for a simple or an intricate life? Living simply is a matter of choice. If we can afford to live a lavish life without compromising our long-term financial goals, then it is our individual discretion to go for it. If we opt for frugality, then we must have a deep reason to institute simplicity. Oftentimes, if we live a simple life, we have less worry and fewer expenses to think about. A simple life doesn't necessarily mean depriving ourselves of the things we deserve and not looking after ourselves in terms of needs.

A decent life doesn't always mean living extravagantly. A simple and decent life would entail having a properly planned life with the basic needs taken care of by our income and not living with debts. We often hear the common phrase, "live within your means", and there is also another thing, which is "live below your means". Obviously, when we try to spend more than what we earn, then we end up having a deficit. And to compensate for our unnecessary spending due to exorbitant prices, we would be submerged in debt.

So how can we live a simple life? Here are some tips that I have personally put into practice in living a simple life.

- Know the important things in your life. If you know what matters, then you are less likely to complicate your life.

- Buy only the things you can afford, don't try to impress other people.

- Stop comparing yourself to others, and don't get jealous of what others have. Just focus on yourself and your own plans. If you get jealous, then you will be tempted to buy or try something beyond your means.

- Celebrate occasions in a simple way. It is good to celebrate, but stick to your budget. If you just do it extravagantly and then keep accumulating debts then for me, that is not a good way to celebrate.

- Choose an economy seat on a flight whenever possible, even if you can afford to be in business class. This can save you a lot of money, the trip is the same anyway.

- Try to recycle and reuse items if possible, to minimize buying new items. This would not only save your money but will also help save carbon emission from manufacturing of these items.

- Be content with an old but working phone, car or anything that you use.

- Walk in the park, not in the mall so you won't be tempted to go into compulsive shopping.

- Learn to cook your own food and try to eat out only occasionally.

- Try to get rid or reduce the number of your credit cards. If you cannot manage it, then there is a possibility that you will incur huge debts.

• Cutting costs on unnecessary things, prudence, or frugality is a good mindset. Be happy with simple things in life.

It's Okay to Say NO

It is human nature to extend help. When our families are in need, we cannot afford to ignore it, especially in emergency or life-and-death situations. If someone approaches us and we can do anything to help, we cannot just close our eyes. Helping is good, but it must be done in the right perspective. If we have the capacity, then it feels better to lend a helping hand. However, if we are too kind and just give in every time someone asks for help without proper assessment, then we are also susceptible to being abused.

Our priority is our families. We can help others, but we don't need to overdo it to the extent that we would be abused, or we just help just to show off that we are generous and kind. Perhaps, many have been into situations of being too kind and being exploited several times. There are some people who would only be nice and treat you like a family when they need you. When you are too generous, they will be closer and exploit you. But when misunderstanding happens out of trivial issues, all your good deeds will be forgotten. From time to time, let us carefully assess every situation before doing any action. Saying NO, may save us emotionally and financially.

In the life of an OFW, sometimes we are perceived to possess more all the time. This may be attributed to misconceptions about what other people can see on social media or simply the general stereotype that if you work abroad, you have a lot of money. If we have hard times, we don't need to always say YES just to please everyone. We can only work within the bounds of our financial capacity.

If we work within your budget for essential family obligations, we can also extend help within our budgetary allocation. If we don't know how to refuse in a nice way, then some situations can be overwhelming, and if it goes out of control, we may encounter worsening financial struggles. Sometimes, it necessitates us to say NO. It is okay to say NO, as long as we genuinely say it with an open heart that we also have our priorities to attend to. Learn to say No in a dignified way and people can understand.

Making a Backup Plan

Are we prepared for any eventual or untoward incidents in our lives? In financial terms, are we ready to face any misfortune and survive if the worst-case scenario takes place? This is where proper planning comes in. Making a contingency plan can be a tool in order to address any unavoidable circumstances and prepare ourselves to hurdle any alarming situation. Making a backup plan or 'Plan B' is necessary in order to have a buffer when things don't go as intended.

Making a back-up plan doesn't need rocket science. It is simply a preparation in intensifying our capacity to mitigate the risks in trying times. It is better to always contemplate on taking a 'calculated risk', in situations concerning our career and financial strength. A plan may vary in terms of strategies, but as long as we commit to employ what we have planned, then it can lessen our burden when a troubling situation comes.

A backup plan can be activated in times of crisis. For example, an unforeseen economic crisis may come in the way leaving the company with no option than to downsize its human resources.

If you're one of those who would lose your job, and you are the breadwinner, how can it impact you and your family? This can result in an unprecedented financial roadblock, where you don't know how to keep sustaining your family's needs if you don't have a backup plan. This calls for a careful assessment of your situation, taking into consideration the risk of losing a job at any time. A backup plan is necessary to overcome any crisis in our financial life. It is good to be prepared.

Learning From Your Mistakes

As human beings, we are prone to make mistakes. Mistakes are inevitable. But what is important is that we learn from our mistakes, and we learn to reflect on the lessons with the hope that we may never commit the same flaws again. It is not about having regrets, but it is about retaining the lessons learned from any shortcomings.

With regards to financial aspects, what are the common mistakes that make us fall prey to troubles and distress?

- Trusting People without knowing them well. Out of kindness and generosity, many of us have experienced being trapped with friends who owe us money as they keep accumulating debt. If it is easy for us to trust them, once they face a problem and are unable to pay, it is to our disadvantage and we lose a huge amount of hard-earned money. We don't need to trust too much, or else we end up chasing people's promises, and it will damage our relationship with someone we engage with. The sad reality is that when you are in trouble, there are still people around who are displaying bitterness instead of showing empathy and compassion.

- Stop Spending on unnecessary things. Suppose you go to a mall or department store and chance upon an attractive item that triggers your impulse, would you buy it or let the urge pass and come back next time? Trying to avoid your habit of being a compulsive shopper is a good strategy to minimize spending on non-essential things. Sometimes, appearances are deceptive, so we have to control our impulses and not get convinced easily by a desire to acquire more items just to satisfy other people's perceptions. Showing off and pretending we can afford expensive things just to impress other people with our success and conspicuous affluence would not be healthy for our finances.

- Avoid taking several credit cards. Proper use of credit cards can be useful but if you have several credit cards and you just splurge on your wants, doing a shopping spree, then time will come that you won't be able to get out from debts. If you have a credit card, use it wisely and be educated on how interest is being calculated, so you won't end up in a financial mess.

- Think several times before investing and don't fall prey to investment scams with sweet promises. Investments are good, but they need to be cautiously evaluated whether they are legitimate or not. For example, if you get enthralled with investments which give you returns that are seemingly "too good to be true", then think a million times about it. Without prudence and cautious action, you will end up losing money from strangers who have strong, convincing power, as if they can move mountains from their promises. Learn to say NO, investment requires deep discernment as you cannot afford to waste your money.

I am sure some of us have our fair share of committing these mistakes, especially from tricks and deception. But we have to realize that our mistakes cannot be reversed. There is no moving backwards and keep on regretting, as we can never turn back time. There are some people who would show empathy but unfortunately some would be in jubilation for our misfortune. This would leave an indelible pain deep inside. We cannot undo the past, but we can use our misgivings as motivation to learn and not make the same mistake in the future. We have to learn our lessons the hard way, and instead of mourning and harbouring ill feelings, we still have time to recover and redeem ourselves from wrong decisions. It is done through resilience, proper planning, perseverance, and a mindset of never losing hope that things will get better as we move forward.

Setting Your Financial Goals

Despite the doom and gloom from our experiences in dealing with finances, we have the power to change our mindset and set a new direction towards financial stability. As we learn from our own dose of ups and downs in terms of financial blunders, we are also in charge of making that leap of faith in deciding to implement changes in the way we think and the way we spend our money. Setting our own goals is important as it will serve as our road map towards the successful achievement of what we aspire for.

If we don't have specific goals with a specified timeline, then we can easily be tempted and misdirected, ending up overspending or incurring debts. There is no standard formula for setting financial goals; we can work on our own budget and requirements. As long as we commit to following our plans religiously, then it may result in beneficial impacts on our finances. We have to create one, and it is uniquely bespoke to our capacity. And what works for one person might be completely different or might not work for another.

In recent months, I have reconnected with a trusted friend who is working as a financial advisor in the Philippines. As we had our conversation, we chanced upon a topic on financial management. He has given me tips on saving and setting financial goals. The first thing he said was, "Know the value of your PhP100 or USD100. If you can allocate it properly, you can get hold of your bigger finances. Second, pay your savings or insurance first (paying yourself first), expenses come second, wants comes third. Then, thirdly, put your money in different baskets. Fourth, control, know what you need and keep it there. And then lastly, he told me to give to charity or tithe."

These tips may resemble that of our own or the generally practiced ones from finance professionals. We can also learn to lay down our plans based on our own experiences and lessons from our mistakes. For instance, personally, I started putting a timeline to pay off my loan and credit card, while having a savings plan on the side starting with a little amount. Then gradually, look for something to invest in to augment my income. I have also ventured on upscaling my talents to hopefully gain a passive income in the future.

For me, it doesn't matter if we move slowly from where we are, and steadily moving forward can empower us to work toward our goals. Hopefully, whatever financial plans we have, if we work consistently and commit to sticking to our plans, no matter what happens, we will be able to reach our dreams in terms of financial stability in due time.

CHAPTER 7

NURTURING YOUR RELATIONSHIPS

A relationship requires a lot of work and commitment."

~ Greta Scacchi

In our existence as human beings, we are truly blessed with good relationships in many ways and forms. As social beings, our life is intertwined with many valuable relationships. Relationship with the creator sets the foundation of it all. In our daily life, we have several social interactions with people around us. We develop and establish relationships, and our relationships serve as fuel and inspiration, as they make us happy to coexist socially or be in harmony with people. However, relationships do not always go smoothly. Conflicts, disagreements and troubles are always part and parcel of any relationship, as we are always subjected to enormous challenges. And considering that we come from different backgrounds and upbringings, altercations and fights are inescapable.

But we can always nurture our relationships, as it needs constant effort, love and commitment to sustain no matter how it costs us. Getting through it requires ardor and adjustments, the ability and willingness to submit and accept our weaknesses with humility. So in stable situations and in the face of challenges, we have to nurture our relationships.

For relationships to grow and bloom, we need to provide what is needed through hard work and commitment. We may have flaws and imperfections, but a relationship is always a work in progress. Continual improvement entails efforts just like development in other aspects of life. The loving relationship needs to be given attention and constant effort. In a relationship, it doesn't always follow that we aspire to maintain a happy state. However, having the courage and dedication to stay connected and survive difficult times is a significant accomplishment in many phases of our relationships.

Relationship with God

In our life, our relationship with the Creator is very important. Our life in itself is a great blessing. With the multitudes of blessings bestowed on us, we are deeply indebted to God's divine power of protecting us, giving us the strength to get through and sustain us despite the many trials. We often ask ourselves, how can we maintain our strong relationship with God? Each of us has a special connection to the ultimate source of our energy, and we have our unique experiences in keeping our close relationship with the Divine.

We may differ in religious practices and traditions, but we attribute it to our personal relationship with God. The way we demonstrate our faith does not necessarily matter. What matters most is we continually surrender and seek guidance from the Creator. We can nurture our relationship with God in our own unique ways. This may include fervent prayers, reflection, meditation, communication and seeking Divine intervention. When we pray deeply, we are talking to God, and communication serves as the gateway to connecting to that ultimate source of energy. Our daily prayers and constant surrender to God serve as our fuel. We pray when we're happy, sad, in a jovial mood and in trying times. And there are no limitations in terms of demonstrating our faith in prayers and reflection. Educating ourselves through the words of God is also a means of knowing God while knowing ourselves as we align to obey His words.

Giving gratitude through serving others is an effective way of nurturing our relationship with God. If we are grateful, then we have the kindness to serve and share our blessings. It can be a source of joy to others. This is also the essence of connecting to Divine Providence.

Being migrant workers, we sometimes find a way to strengthen our faith through the community we associate with in worshipping God. For example, devoting time to attending church services or prayers can solidify our connection. Prayers are very powerful. From a distance where we are always flooded with worries and challenges, fervent prayer is a great way of comforting ourselves. When we are weary, we find solace in prayers. Strong faith in prayers is our weapon to overcome obstacles in life, keeping our faith in trying times can fuel our perseverance with the hope that we can always thrive and get better.

Relationship With Family

Our family is the reason why we work hard every day. They are our inspiration to keep moving forward, giving us a sense of confidence and belongingness. Every day, as we juggle, we look forward to connecting with our families for strength and motivation. Our family is our strength and, at the same time, a reason for our weakness. When things go wrong and our family is in troubling situations, we are also bothered and we cannot function well if we don't put things in proper perspective.

Maintaining a strong connection with our spouse, our children and other family members is vital in making us feel loved, comfortable and energized. Without a connection to our families, we may feel lost and depressed. It is essentially a major part of our overall well-being and mental health. It affects our mood and our disposition at work if there are any issues or differences within the family. Communication is very important to maintain a harmonious relationship and avoid escalating things to an uncontrollable scale. As a family, good communication is necessary. Being a good listener and understanding the sensibilities or needs of your partner or any family member plays a pivotal role in maintaining a good relationship.

Cultivating the values, culture and commitment to a shared family goal can strengthen the relationship. This means that both parties are aligned with the vision and the greater purpose of why you venture on a decision. Our family is our anchor, and maintaining good communication and connection with our family is one of the keys to nurturing better relationships. We have to appreciate each family member as our treasure. Prioritizing our family needs is our happiness.

Distance is not an obstacle to staying connected with our family. Effective communication plays a crucial role in the life of a migrant worker separated miles away from their families. Keeping the bond and connection with clear communication and setting the right rules amenable to all parties is a step to stabilizing the relationship. Respect and trust in the partner, for example, are big contributing factors to waning away undesirable issues that can jeopardize the relationship. As long as each party is willing to understand and always propagate kindness, then family relationships can certainly prosper.

Resolving Conflicts

Have you been into some arguments and misunderstandings with family, friends or anyone recently? Have you been wronged or provoked by anyone? How did you resolve some conflicts that you have experienced? For as long as we exist and interact with people, there is always a possibility of disagreement and differing viewpoints. We are raised in different ways, and disagreements and conflicts cannot be avoided. We have our own frame of mind and disposition. The way we think, speak and behave may not do well with others and no matter how we strive to have a peaceful co-existence, there are times when we cannot control ourselves and can utter abrasive words if we are provoked, and that can cause friction.

Conflicts and misunderstandings can occur within our family, in the workplace, with friends, or within our inner circle. This can happen at any time because the dynamics of our interaction are constantly changing since we are dealing with diverse personalities.

If you have some petty quarrel with your spouse or friend, would you fix it quickly, or would you wait for the right time to make the first move to resolve the issue? We have varying approaches and strategies to tackle our differences and misunderstandings with people we interact with. Some of us may wait for emotions to subside and talk things out in a rational and prudent way so as not to aggravate the situation. Some of us may have a resolute resolve and may act quickly by talking to those we are in conflict with, hoping for a quick fix and not sleeping over any issue.

I have gone through different conflicts and misunderstandings, too, in personal and professional areas of my life. I have my own dose of sleepless nights, trying to figure out when the conflict will be over and have a peaceful resolution. But I have learned a lot and some of these tips have been effective in resolving issues in my own experiences.

- Know what you want, whether you opt for peace or you want to prolong the conflict. If you know what you want, then the actions will follow the predominant thought in your mind.

- Reflect and pray for guidance that you will be sensitive to other people's feelings, not throw hurtful words, and deepen the conflict. Reflect on the times someone has helped you and not selfishly considering your fallacious anger.

- Stop overthinking and eliminate your hesitation to talk to the person you have a quarrel with. Don't live with "what ifs".

- Be humble to approach the other party. Humility is very important. For me, most of the time, I initiate moves to talk to the concerned party, regardless if I'm the offended party or the other way around. However, there is also a limit to whether someone is filled to the brim with pride and vengeance.

- Admit your mistakes and lower your pride. I have experienced this; when I admit my mistakes, it would soften the heart of the other party and also do the same. And when both of us acknowledge our mistakes, then the path towards peaceful resolution is at hand.

- Be kind to forgive and be honest to ask for forgiveness if you offend the other party. Learn to unplug and unload animosities.

- Don't be confrontational, just talk in a calm and respectful manner. Don't dwell on the past, avoid rhetorics in bringing up recycled issues and unresolved differences.

• Learn to listen and not judge the other person right away without giving him/her time to explain.

• Don't think that you are superior to others. Be compassionate and put yourself in the other person's situation.

• Think about the value of the person, your commitment, the cherished moments you have shared and the beneficial impacts of your relationship.

Keeping and Valuing Friends

In our life, we have several sets of friends. We know from deep within that we have our definition of best friend, trusted friend and the like. And we know for a fact that having a good friend is a blessing. Friends are people we are connected with, those we can depend on and run to at times. Every time we have good or bad news, we always tell our close friends aside from our families. When something goes wrong, we cannot hide it from our trusted friends. They are our shining armour in times of trouble and adversities in life.

Friendship paints vibrant colours in our journey. They are a significant part of our life's milestones. We celebrate successes with friends in the same way that we seek emotional refuge and empathy with them in our failures and trials. Quantity of friends is not the defining characteristic of how comfortable and happy we are with our friendship. But it is the quality of friends that matters most. We can have few but dependable and true friends, friends that will stay loyal no matter what happens, friends who are never judgemental but will always be understanding even if we wronged them. When we have problems, sharing them with good friends can help us unload some burdens and make us feel better.

Just like any other relationship, friendship is also subjected to varying forms of trials. There are times when friendship can be put to the test, and in some cases, we are almost at the edge, which can even result in losing some friends. But for as long as we know the value and we stay connected to the happy memories and good learning experiences with our friends, then we know they are worth keeping. There are friends who are like our siblings or family, and there are friends who are just one message away when we need them the most. Some friends are truly our treasures, who are selfless, and always ready to come to the rescue when we are in difficult situations. Their value cannot be underestimated, they cry, laugh and fight for us. True friends appreciate our value, support us in our endeavours and are willing to stand up for us without expectations in return.

So it is equally important to keep your friends while gaining new ones. How do we keep or maintain our connection with our friends? There are many ways and we know our friends well. We understand their characteristics and we have our unique bonds with different types of friends.

Maintaining good communication is key to staying connected with our friends. Nowadays, communication can be done in a snap and at the tip of our fingers with the advent of technology. Personal interaction is important, but we don't have to see each other often to get connected. Distance is not a limiting factor when reaching out to our friends. If we truly know our friends, even if we have been separated by distance for decades, the bond is still there, and we don't lose track in knowing that deep inside, we know who our real friends are. Perhaps you have that one friend whom you haven't seen for so long, but your conversation can go deeper with the same bond as if you just met yesterday.

We can have different ways of keeping the bond with our friends. Having good conversations and rekindling the good old days, staying loyal, and being happy for our friend's achievements are vital in maintaining strong friendships. To keep good friends, we need to start from ourselves. Understanding our own strengths and weaknesses will help us understand our friends as well. Keeping a good heart and being a good company will also transcend to others. When we have positive vibrations that radiate from deep within, we can also attract and gain new friends. Good character and a happy mindset will magnetize people in our community, workplace, or circle, and in the process, it would become an avenue to gain new friends.

Despite some unavoidable arguments and misunderstanding from petty issues, let us try to reflect on the essential value of our friends. Friends come and go, but real friends will stay connected no matter what happens. There are times that friendship fades and is painted with intrigues, and there are some inevitable changes in the way we are treated by them. If the transformation is beneficial, then it is an opportune time to break free from the misconception that our friends are exclusive.

It is a good sign of maturity to be flexible and be adaptive to positive changes. In the end, it is important to propagate kindness and understanding and move forward realizing that friendship is a significant part of our mundane existence.

The Importance of Good Communication

In any relationship, establishing good communication plays a pivotal role in maintaining bonds and connections. Effective communication is a great tool for bridging the gap and maintaining a healthy relationship. It can be a relationship with our spouse, children, best friend, close friend or other family members. It is natural that in our relationships, we go through rough patches and trying times. The best way to resolve and regain that bond is not to instill negative rhetoric but to communicate in a positive and constructive way.

How do we communicate effectively? Why is good communication important? When we communicate explicitly, we express our feelings, and we try to make ourselves understood by delivering the right message. We can start by being true to ourselves and authentic in expressing what we feel. In the same manner, we try to listen and understand the feelings being expressed by the other party. If we don't listen and react defensively, then it can lead to more confusion. When there is misunderstanding, communicating well is not just talking, it is expressing genuinely, listening attentively and saying things with prudence so as not to add more dissension to the worsening situation.

Effective communication is important because when we are being clear and understood, we can also capture other people's needs. If we know what we expect, we have to understand their needs and expectations, too. Communication is a give-and-take scheme in a healthy relationship. It will strengthen and enhance understanding and connection because when you communicate effectively, you will freely express your emotions without the fear of being judged and without the apprehension of being criticized. It will make strong bonds and connections as you happily communicate and talk things out, resolving an issue and showing empathy in troubling situations.

One personal example of maintaining good communication

may be related to other Filipino migrant workers who are in the same situation. Personally, I have learned that maintaining good communication in a long-distance relationship with your spouse is very important in resolving misunderstandings, issues and conflicts. For instance, when I have some personal quarrel and arguments with my husband, the best way to resolve it is to communicate effectively rather than let feelings and opinions be left undelivered.

Miscommunication can lead to the accumulation of issues, aggravating the situation. Instead of just ignoring the issue, you can talk it out with honesty and have the ability to listen to your partner. Enhancing your communication skills, keeping the communication channel open, and expressing your feelings with respect and rationality will help you weather whatever issue. This will lead to a peaceful resolution and mutual understanding that will strengthen your relationship.

Trusting Your Instincts

Not all relationships are beneficial. Things and issues that transpire in a relationship can sometimes become harmful and negatively affect our well-being. There are some relationships flooded with issues beyond our control or influence. It can become toxic and degrade our ability to move forward.

In handling relationships, there are times that compel us to listen to our instincts. Relationships can be subjected to any hurdle and hardships. Sometimes, it takes us to listen to our gut feelings to see if a relationship is still healthy and worth keeping or if a decision must be made.

This is the time that we have to explore the use of our intuition because, in reality, some relationships won't work. Instead of being our refuge, it may become our burden and cause for depression. That's why we need some point of introspection or reflection as to the state of our relationship, and in the process, we would discern and decide. Trusting our instincts and our gut feeling through listening to that inner voice, humbly admitting the fact that some relationships require a much-needed break while keeping the lessons learned in a positive and constructive way.

Be Kind and Forgiving

At any point in our lives and in our interactions with different people, irreconcilable differences may arise that can cause a scar in any relationship. Different situations call for different strategies that will test our patience and character. Sometimes, we can be the offending party, or sometimes, we can be wronged. There are unavoidable turn of events that can make people harsh, without the intention to hurt us, but in the process, leaving us pain and suffering.

Being kind and forgiving is a positive trait that we can maintain in propagating a healthy relationship. To nurture our relationship, we need not be right at all times. Even if we are the offended party, we can choose to be kind and extend forgiveness to those who are remorseful. Forgiving is not an act of being inferior or showing weakness. It demonstrates strength and humility that we opt for peace and don't want to prolong the agony of a broken bond.

Having a positive mindset and disposition in showing kindness in the face of challenges can transform us into a better person. Even if there are irreconcilable differences, we can wait for the right timing until we patch things up, but at least we have already forgiven and settled issues starting from our inner self.

Unravelling the power of kindness and forgiveness is a powerful way to maintain healthy relationships. With the realization that even when we are gone from this world, we leave behind a legacy of imbibing kindness and selflessness through the examples we set through our relationships.

Forgiving others can be a great gesture of kindness. In this world, spreading love and kindness is needed as we are faced with conflicts and misunderstanding. If we are magnanimous, we can create strong bonds within our relationships. It will pave the way for peace, unity and understanding as we aim for healthier and happier life.

GETTING THROUGH AND GROWING

"Without continual growth and progress, such words as improvement, achievement, and success have no meaning"

~ Benjamin Franklin

When we are thrown outside our comfort zones, we have to adjust to the new environment and different sets of challenges. But it is our nature to continue striving hard for survival. And as we engage with the many complex situations, our character is put to a test, whether we get through and continue our quest for growth. Getting through any obstacle entails perseverance and ardour, as we have been exposed to different experiences in life. They make us strong and resilient, and with a resilient mindset, we can get out stronger and overcome obstacles.

Painstakingly staying course with what we aim for in life can be daunting, especially when we are subjected to troubling situations. The first thing to do in order to toughen our capabilities is a decision from our inner self to follow through with what we laid down. With strong conviction, we won't give up no matter what comes in the way to test our patience and persistence.

Getting Through Career Challenges

In the case of Filipino migrant workers, as we settle in the foreign land we are already confronted with many difficulties. One reason that we decided to try our luck in another country is the possibility to thrive in our chosen career. But we are not offered with silver platters; we have to exert extra effort to weather any challenges in our career life.

What are some common challenges you have experienced as OFW? Perhaps many would agree that most of us have gone through nightmares in our job search journey. The first challenge that we need to hurdle is how to secure that first job and prove that we are a worthy candidate to be chosen. We face the usual anxiety during a job interview when our experiences and inclination to the position are being questioned.

Preparation is a significant tool for studying the company, having an adequate review of the veracity of the information we write, and being mentally prepared to have a constructive exchange of views during the interview. It is important to be calm and be ourselves, not trying to overrate and exaggerate our answers. Being true to yourself can be manifested in your facial expressions and knowledge, which are very important in getting through and nailing that first job interview. When you can hurdle this challenge, then you can breathe a sigh of relief that you have the chance to work on yourself and upgrade for a better future.

When we land a job in a new working environment, we need a lot of effort to prove our worth by highlighting our skills, knowledge and capabilities that will place us ahead of the game. We have to keep up with the challenge in making adjustments and gaining the trust and confidence of our superiors, our colleagues and blend in a new workplace culture in order to fulfill our responsibilities excellently. Proving our worth through hard work entails breaking that limiting belief that resides in our minds. Being optimistic and convincing ourselves that we can do the tasks with confidence. Breaking the barrier, changing our mindset, and having that "can do" attitude with an open mind for learning is a significant way to feel secure on the job.

There may be hard times in the job as we aim to progress in our careers. But if we keep our focus on growth and not on the negativities encountered, then we can certainly achieve career progression. If we have a positive mindset, then we can play our role well and even go beyond what our assigned task is. Being positive is a prelude to being productive because if you feel and propagate positivity at work, there is no space for obstructive thoughts that can hinder productivity. If we are productive, we sometimes forget that time is passing, and we never get tired of connecting and cooperating with our colleagues, which is the essence of achieving our common goals through unity and teamwork.

Sometimes, we will be faced with trials and challenging times upon meeting the expectations of our superiors. However, let us not be discouraged that even in the most demanding job, we still come out stronger and better. We have to capitalize on our strengths, skills and knowledge to overcome any hindrance and work for continual improvements. We have to ignore negative impressions and gossip that can diminish our positive energy at work. In doing so, we focus on our productivity with optimism.

Developing Your Skills

When we are given an opportunity, we don't just relax and become complacent. If we want to improve our situation, we need to develop our skills. We are blessed with unique talents and possess different skill sets. With the many challenges ahead of us, being flexible and ready to adapt to any situation at work calls for improvement in many areas of our career life. There are many ways to develop our skills as we gain years of experience at work. The most important thing is that we understand and know the importance of education. Continuously developing our skills evokes a competitive edge in our respective fields. If we recognise the fact that our knowledge is not enough, then we always embrace a good learning attitude.

I can recall my own experience when I started my fledgling career in the field of Environment and Sustainability. I didn't know where to start learning and it seemed that I was just groping in the dark and had no idea whether I would survive. My Managers and mentor told me to pick things up as I go along every day and to never stop learning in the practical way, which means from practical onsite application and not only based on theories. From there, I developed an eagerness to learn whatever I would encounter on site and slowly built up my confidence to tackle the technical aspects of the job as time passed by.

So, how do you upgrade your skills? Here are some ways that we can try to develop our skills and enable growth for career improvement.

- Admit that you still don't know many things about your job, and be open to feedback from others.

- Assess your skills and areas for improvement and try to learn every day.

- Have an open mind and seek help from your senior colleagues or mentors who are more experienced to give you guidance and direction.

- Don't be afraid to take risks in trying new tasks.

- If you are given additional work, don't complain, but treat that as an opportunity to learn new things.

- Set your goals and the level you want to reach.

- Minimize unnecessary online activities and increase time exposure to free educational and informational materials and videos.

- Grab the opportunity to attend training and skills enhancement programs.

- Be optimistic and never stop learning. If you have adequate knowledge, you have an advantage.

Having Excellent Performance and Constantly Improving

Having a job is a great blessing that we have to take care of. But in our workplace, being a performer is not an easy road to take. It entails hard work, perseverance and a mindset to constantly improve in whatever task we do. Giving our best shot requires focus and willpower to overcome any obstacle and difficult situations in fulfilling our responsibilities. It doesn't matter if we commit mistakes or we have shortcomings, as long as we try to correct our mistakes and learn the lessons so that they may not happen again. Failures are our great teachers, and from failing, we can be strong and resilient to stand up and keep the motivation to work hard in order to succeed. Even if things go slow, we should keep moving forward and get out of complacency and indolence. Slow progress is better than being stagnant and just sleeping in our disappointments.

So, what does it take to be an excellent performer? It is a given fact that we are already blessed with knowledge and acquired skills. However, being an excellent performer requires extra effort and the ability to possess the qualities to tackle challenges towards excellence. If we want to excel, look at excellent people and try to learn and emulate their actions and good qualities that are significantly contributing to achieving great performance. It takes extraordinary efforts, continuous learning, and possessing good qualities such as confidence, focus, perseverance, consistency and a positive mindset. These are good to know, but words and theories without actual application will never come to fruition and be instrumental in achieving our goals.

Let me discuss some situations where one can excel at work. For example, in the workplace, we all have our job descriptions and targets detailed in Key Performance Indicators (KPIs), where each employee is assigned a specific target to be achieved in a particular timeline. The first thing we should do is know our targets and evaluate our abilities and strategies to fulfil them. Once we define our action plans, then focus and consistency are needed in our daily actions geared towards achieving and even going beyond the target.

If we want to be excellent and ahead of the game, we need to set our goals not on a fixed number but exceeding what is expected from us. Being consistent would mean ignoring the negativities and just focusing on our daily actions and productivity. We should be a team player and not be a distraction to other team members. Focusing on yourself doesn't mean being self-centred. We have to cooperate and help others, but we must focus on being productive and reject the culture of gossiping about other colleagues' performance.

At work, procrastination is a big hindrance. As much as possible, if we know that we have a deadline to beat, we don't need to relax and wait for the deadline to start doing our task. It cannot be denied that we become sluggish and unmotivated sometimes but always try to look for inspiration. For instance, as migrant workers, we make sacrifices for our families and our self-fulfilment, so we should not rest on our laurels but continue to work hard to overcome mediocrity and become excellent performers in our chosen fields. As we are called for this unusual career journey, we have to explore strategies to excel in the workplace while encouraging others to be high performers and continually seek opportunities for improvement.

Surviving in Your Working Environment

In my experience, there is no perfect workplace. But we are not here to look for perfection; we are here for improvement in terms of personal, financial and professional aspects of our lives. Dealing with different people demands adjustment and the right mindset to triumph over challenges in the performance of our job. There is no standard equation for surviving and keeping yourself contented and happy at work. But whatever the circumstances, we have to get through it and successfully survive, trying to do our best and excel.

Every day in our workplace, a chain of events and our working environment may test our patience and survival power. We may have gone through some uncomfortable situations as we associate and interact with our superiors, colleagues and other employees. We have our own share of horrible days and dispositions which may affect other people around us. In the same manner, we can get affected by the contagious negativity of other people who are fond of complaining and venting out unpalatable words. There are also instances of feeling undervalued, which may consume our self-esteem. Others may have also experienced being ignored and not given importance due to insecurities felt by other colleagues or superiors. But these are not reasons enough to stumble and become unproductive. We have to preserve our integrity and continually improve even if we seem to be unknown to others.

When there are days that you are swarmed with frustrations, intrigues, criticisms and negative vibrations, what would you do? This scenario can happen to anyone, and as we are emotionally and professionally equipped with capabilities, we can become stronger and better. We should not be onion-skinned to criticism and feedback, as we need them as external eyes to push us to move forward and get better every day. If we only exist in a comfortable situation, then we will be complacent and think that everything is going well, preventing us from constantly practising until we overcome inferiority.

There are also times when we are clouded with doubts in the workplace. In times of uncertainty, let us try to trust our gut feelings and not rely on others because some people may not have the same intentions as we do. Amidst the negativity, we should spread compassion, positivity and a cheerful disposition. By rejecting unnecessary distractions and unhealthy discussions, we can eliminate the room for frustration and resentment. Then, we focus on our journey to survive and create a positive and productive professional experience.

Inspiring Others

More often than not, we all need inspiration. We need

motivation and constant push, especially when we are confronted with numerous challenges. In terms of professional life, how can we be an inspiration in the workplace? There are many ways that we can resonate inspiring energy to others. Being a good performer with unwavering commitment and dedication to fulfil our responsibilities can be a source of inspiration.

As we spend a considerable period of time in the workplace, let us try to explore these simple ways to inspire our colleagues and other employees. Starting your morning at work with a smile and greeting everyone you meet is a positive way to kickstart a great work day. When others can see our positive attitude and we stop complaining and treat our colleagues nicely, then this will echo into propagating more positivity and good vibrations.

In an era where the workplace requires us to be contentious in this competitive world, excellent performance is a significant parameter in gaining respect and building good credibility. And if we establish good credibility by being conscientious in performing our job, others will look up to us. We can extend help and assist others whenever they need us the most, being a good team player. Helping others can spread kindness and a selfless attitude, which is an indication that you have the confidence to be a model and plausible among your peers worthy of emulation. If we set a good example for others, we can be ahead of the game by fostering a positive and collaborative work culture, and in doing so, they will also be inspired to improve continually and become better.

Despite the many twists and paradoxes in life, we can also inspire friends and other people who need encouragement to endure their situation. As a personal example, there are many occasions where other OFWs reach out for motivation, fighting against homesickness and some cases of challenging situations.

And I would simply tell them to continue being hopeful, connect to their biggest WHY, and continue to pray that things would get better. Words of encouragement would inspire other people and never underestimate the power of words as they can provide a trigger to regain motivation and positivity.

Lifelong Learning in Career Development

Education is a powerful tool in our career growth and overall development. As we embark on our career journey, using our knowledge and skills as well as the education in our chosen fields are essential towards career advancement. In order to progress, we have to embrace the fact that it is always a continuous learning process. We learn from our mistakes and through constant practice, we learn the best strategy to overcome challenges in our career.

As we aim to progress and climb up the ladder to success, commitment to continuous learning and professional development is vital. If we aspire to improve our situation, let us realize the importance of staying updated and relevant in an ever-evolving professional landscape in our field of specialization. Most companies have career development programs that can aid us in developing our skill sets. At work, nobody is indispensable. But when we enhance our capabilities and are equipped with extensive knowledge, skills, and talents, then we may feel secure. "Knowledge is power" as they say.

In my professional journey as an example, these strategies have been instrumental in achieving my career goals.

• Defining my targets and my timeline.

• I have the eagerness to learn and improve my strengths.

- Attending courses to gain knowledge and learn new skills that relate to my position.

- Investing in training and other educational platforms.

- Completing relevant certificate programs to improve my resume.

- Attending conferences and events to gain knowledge and experience.

- Watching educational as well as motivational videos to augment my practical learning.

- Continually looking for opportunities to learn and hone my skills.

- Be open minded, agile and continually embrace new technology and innovative ideas to be efficient at work.

Our growth's backbone can also be attributed to our consistent actions and not to talents and skills alone. It is not a measure of how we start but how we persist and stay on course to finish the race. In life, we have the power to set the direction of our destiny. It is not a preordained fate, but wherever we go and whatever we become, it is a work in progress.

CHAPTER 9

MAINTAINING POSITIVITY

"Choose to be optimistic, it feels better."

~ Dalai Lama

What is feeling positive? Does it mean the absence of negative thoughts? Every day, it doesn't always go that our predominant thoughts are positive. Feeling positive doesn't necessarily mean the absence of negativity but rather an optimistic feeling that whatever happens, you will triumphantly overcome any obstacle and come out better. It is a sensation bearing a positive mindset that things will be alright. Feeling positive is a happy feeling deep within us. This means that negative emotions exist, but we don't allow the frustration or negativity to topple us down.

In this fast-paced world, how do you set the feeling for the day? Is it a cheerful day with a happy countenance or a gloomy day with a miserable feeling? Having the ability of praising other people rather than criticizing propagates happiness. It is vitally important to spread love and positivity in our workplace, home or in family. But as human beings, it is inevitable that we sometimes succumb to negativity. We tend to be discouraged, especially in overwhelming situations of trials and distresses.

If we are already bewildered, filling our mind with optimism and positive thinking can be grueling from deep within. Sometimes if we don't control our mind it becomes an emotional upheaval that goes beyond thoughts that can result in impulsive actions.

Keeping the Positive Energy

How do you start your day, feeling lethargic or energetic? Our energy level is not constantly high at all times. With our hectic schedule considering the dynamics of our personal and professional lives, it cannot be denied that our energy can shrink at any time. But starting our day with a positive outlook can make a difference. If we start from our thoughts, they will be felt in our hearts, and they will be displayed in our facial expressions. If we feel good, we also possess the energy that can beneficially impact other people whom we associate with. Positive energy is contagious and has a multiplier effect; it resonates with other people with a positive impact.

Sustaining positive energy is a challenge. Even on a daily basis, when things get rough, we can lose our minds and succumb to the abyss of negativity. It is very important to start with positive affirmation, telling ourselves first thing in the morning that we are feeling good and good things will unfold unto us. The power of positive words we verbalize can trigger a feeling of strength from within that makes us ready to wrestlle with any challenging situation. Even if we are confronted with inappropriate behaviours from other people, if we start being positive, destructive emotions cannot infiltrate our core.

Suppose you are given a choice, would you carry a lighter or a heavy heart? Starting our day with a heavy heart would proliferate the gloomy countenance that can make us repulsive instead of attracting good vibes and good things. To counter such despondency, we have to kick start our day with optimism and imbibe positivity to power through. And if we gravitate to positivity, we would immerse ourselves in victory from the smallest issues to significantly greater concerns in our personal and professional lives.

Ignore the Negativity

If there is positivity, there is also an opposing side which is negativity. But how do we deal with negativity? It is rampant everywhere, even from our inner self, and there is always a negative feeling or pessimism. Sometimes, we create our own enemy from deep within. And around us, there are countless negative emotions we can encounter from different people and situations. When we are swamped with discouragement and antagonism, we can still come out better if we are equipped with the right emotional faculties to deal with negative thinking.

No matter how happy we are, we will be exposed to unhappy and miserable people around us. Unhappy people are envious and are not content with what they have and they keep chasing possessions even beyond their reach. Some go to the extent of stepping into the rights of other people just to satisfy their desires. Being happy with who you are and what you have is a great starting point in maintaining positivity. If you try to obliterate negative feelings, start cleansing yourself and shut the door on envy and jealousy.

If we are confronted with inappropriate judgment and criticism, can we still stand our ground unaffected? For example, in the lives of OFWs, we may be subjected to negative impressions painted against us. Some would cast doubt on surviving our relationships, some would question why we chose this kind of life and set-up, some would question our ability to get through and achieve our ambitions, and some would even laugh at us. We have to focus on good things and don't mind the naysayers or those who always try to defame us.

Let us accept the fact that people have different character and opinion. No matter how kind we are, no matter how good we treat others, criticism and negative comments are unavoidable.

For some, it is normal to throw unsavoury comments. Perhaps, it is in their vein and it becomes a systemic toxicity. The best reaction is to ignore the negativity and the unnecessary distractions will just die a natural death.

Fighting against negative feelings starts from our inner self. If we think and feel negative, it can also manifest in our attitude, and the best way to shun that feeling is to think of good things and blessings in many aspects of our lives. Strive to fight the negativity from deep inside and it will bring out the positive aura externally. Every day, we have the power to defy negativity, and we have to choose the people we spend most of our time with because they influence our perspective. If we associate with an optimistic circle, then there is a snowball effect of positive energy.

Keeping the Faith

Have you tried walking in the dark? What keeps you moving to see the light? Most of us, in trying times, keep our faith and look forward to getting things better despite the fact that we are almost on the brink of losing that thin line of hope. Faith is our anchor, and faith is based on our personal conviction that in our hearts, there has to be some light at the end of darkness.

It is easy to lose grip on what we believe in, especially when things go crazy and we don't know how to process our emotions amidst the trials. And if we succumb to losing our faith, we can be tempted to go astray, trying to divert our attention from our problems and end up aggravating the issue in the long run. In times like this, we can harness the power of our unshakeable faith and making it stronger to withstand any obstacles. To triumph entails tiny steps geared towards strengthening the anchor that binds our self-awareness and having that faith to sustain us.

What does having strong faith mean for OFWs? As Filipino migrant workers, we have always been deluged with many challenges and difficulties in many aspects of our professional and personal lives. Sometimes, we can be overwhelmed and entertain the idea of giving up. For example, some of us are undergoing many problems in terms of career stability and incessantly seeking the best opportunity. Some may feel hopeless and depressed about their situation. But let us remind ourselves to revive and strengthen our faith that God is preparing the right opportunity and something better for us.

When we seemingly feel alone and we traverse the uncertainties of life, faith is our fuel to keep moving forward amidst difficulties. It is essential not to lose track of our direction and our true purpose with genuine intention. With faith, we can certainly overcome any trial and can triumphantly soar high.

Practising Gratitude

One great way to maintain positivity is by being grateful. Practising gratitude can instigate a good feeling from deep within.

It is one of the greatest virtues to live by. But what really is gratitude? In simple words, gratitude means "the state of being grateful", as defined by the Merriam-Webster Dictionary. Acknowledging that we have been endowed with something beneficial in our life spreads a positive feeling within us. Expressing gratitude instantly makes us feel better internally. Gratitude takes us to a blissful state while feeling grateful for what we have been blessed with—something we receive or experience that may include tangible things, good deeds or acts, advices, lessons, gifts of talents, experiences, and memories, among others, that we come across as we journey through life.

How to be grateful? The first thing is to be mindful and reflect on our blessings. When we assess ourselves introspectively despite the many ups and downs, it reminds us of the multitude of reasons to be grateful for. The best starting point is a profound appreciation to the Creator for the gift of life. Being alive is in itself the greatest gift that we must be thankful for, and we move forward with the grit that no matter what comes our way, we will always have the courage to keep going and never give up. Being grateful for the life we have can make us grow in the tenets of continual improvement despite the many starts and stops in our journey. We should be thankful for always being blessed with God's protection, magnanimity and loving embrace.

There are countless things that we can be truly grateful for. Being blessed with the genuine care, love, and dedication of our parents, spouses, children, family, and friends is one of the things we truly treasure in life. Let us not forget to give thanks to people who have helped us get through difficulties in life, those with unequivocal kindness who have extended assistance to support our education, especially when we were struggling. We are also equally grateful to our teachers who moulded us with knowledge and values that significantly contributed to who we become.

As a Filipino migrant worker in Dubai, I am grateful every day for God's constant protection of me and my family and for my enduring strength. I am deeply grateful for the opportunity to be a resident in one of the best cities in the world and auspiciously be safe in UAE as one of the world's safest countries. The gift of employment that enables me to provide for my family and share some blessings with those in dire need is worthy of appreciation. The diversity of careers offered by this country has been helpful in significantly improving our economic situation and detaching a little from the bondage of poverty.

Despite the many challenges, we appreciate life's simple pleasures and always embrace the mantra that life is still beautiful. And no matter how bad our situation can be, we always hope for brighter days ahead. When we appreciate what we have, it inspires us to recognize that life is worth living and sharing with others.

On the other hand, when we express gratitude vocally, it gives us pleasant gratification that dissipates into our system, thereby converting our desolation into a joyful state. When we fill our hearts with gratitude, we can easily ignore negativity and refrain from having regrets, and it drives us to do more for others while continually trying to become better. Having a grateful heart opens an opportunity for more blessings and good things to unfold.

Choosing to Be Happy

Life in itsef is enigmatic. It is full of uncertainties, absurdities and events beyond our control and comprehension. Undesirable things and frustrations make our feelings unpleasant and can stir up a range of reactions, such as being upset, infuriated, and depressed. Even in unpredictable events, we can have the power to control our reaction and slowly shift that despairing mood into a happy state. Our happiness comes from ourselves. It is not dependent on external factors, but genuine happiness is a personal possession. It depends on how we set our frame of mind. It is a personal affair and personal state of mind and it must be felt from within, not on wishful thinking but for real.

How can we choose to be happy? Genuine happiness starts with a positive frame of mind and then the joyful feeling emanates from deep within. It depends on how we decide and make a choice that despite the depressing and unfavourable conditions, we should continue to look at the positive perspective. Being happy doesn't mean there is no space for sadness and desolation. It simply means that even in the most disheartening episodes in our lives, we don't let sadness and disappointment consume us.

It is alright to feel the pain and mourn but it is not beneficial to be sad for a long period of time. There has to be a limit and we have to realize that things happen because it implies something deeper that gives us life's lessons. In times like we are about to give up, we have to compose ourselves and stand up. Being our own cheer leader is essentially needed for us to have that strength to carry on.

Every day is a chance and a choice to be happy. When we start our day with positive affirmation and a positive outlook, the blissful energy makes us more productive and aligned with our bigger mission to make a difference. Let that choice to stay happy be a vibrant glow that lights up the long, winding road as we journey through life. Staying happy is vital in staying connected with things that really matter in our lives. We cannot choose what's bestowed upon us, but we have the power to discern how we react and accept things as they come. In the process of finding that inspiration from ourselves, it transcends into a greater being and radiates that exuberance to people around us.

To be truly happy entails acceptance and being content in life. If we continue to be insatiable, especially in material aspirations, then we can be in an unhappy state. A joyful heart is instrumental in spreading love and compassion. If you are a happy person, you will shun jealousy and always find time to cheer people up, even when you are struggling. Spreading happiness, even in simple gestures like a smile, can uplift people to propel positive energy, love and compassion.

Despite the many challenges in life, let us be happy and contented with our blessings. Happiness can drive away stress and sickness and can boost our immunity. Maintaining a healthy lifestyle, being joyful and kind will improve our overall well-being. Let us choose love over hate and happiness over sadness, and life will be beautiful and fulfilling.

CHAPTER 10

ACHIEVING YOUR DREAMS

"A dream doesn't become reality through magic; it takes sweat, determination and hard work."

~ Colin Powell

We all have our dreams and aspirations in life. We may have varying situations and different levels in our journey. Either we are on hiatus, on track or temporarily lost track of our goals, but one thing for certain is that the roads we are taking are directed towards achieving our dreams at our own pace.

In our journey, we are always subjected to many challenging and troubling times. There are always roadblocks and setbacks, but nothing can stop us from continually pursuing our goals, no matter how difficult it is. If we constantly implement actions with ardour and robust belief, we can certainly overcome obstacles and reach the final destination where sacrifices are paid off. If we look at the bigger picture, our goals are not solely for our satisfaction, but it is our fulfilment to be instrumental in the overall development of those who depend on us. And above all, transforming our dreams into reality is a sense of fulfilment for the relentless toil for the glory of our Creator.

What is Your Definition of Success

In everything we do, we always want to succeed. More often than not, no one aims to fail in any endeavour. How do we define success? Some of us may think of success as a standard measure in terms of bigger possessions, huge achievements, and success factors in terms of numbers. In a general sense, success is an achievement of a desired outcome or fulfilment of an aim. We regard success in many ways and through many attributes. Some may gauge it by reaching the pinnacle of success in terms of financial stability and professional achievements.

But success is not just defined by the perspective of attaining big things, huge numbers and reaching that peak. It is an achievement of your planned goals in small milestones and getting through something that gives you a sense of fulfilment in your undertakings. It can be experienced in little things and it depends on how we look at it objectively.

Every day is a success in a multitude of ways. In our daily lives, whatever we get through for a specific period of time can be executed in our action plans in personal, relationships, or professional aspects. Any progress is a form of success. The moment we wake up and go out there taking on the challenge of fulfilling our duties and responsibilities conscientiously gives us a sense of good feeling. Small things count and cannot be underestimated. When we bounce back and are resilient every time we experience setbacks, that's already victoriously standing up and striving to get better.

How can we attain success? Whether in small or big things, we need to have plans that are executed with unwavering dedication and consistency. When we start to commit to our plans and goals, then it is itself a significant milestone that gives us energy and a positive frame of mind to continually take on the challenge of reaching the destination we aspire for. In the process of getting better, everyone is guided by that vision of making a difference in our lives and creating an impact in the lives of other people.

Setting Your Goals

Have you tried walking without direction and having no predetermined point of destination in your mind? Or driving a car without planning where to go? We may have experienced this in our lives when we were just pointing to nowhere without going in the right direction. Then, we easily stumble and fall into traps because we don't carry a solid foundation of staying on course towards a clear destination. If we don't know where to go, then we might just start with no sense of purpose, making the journey easily doomed in the face of adversity.

Setting our goals is an important first step if we want to achieve something. It serves as a guiding star and strategic plan as we traverse our way towards achieving our dreams. Having the vision to set specific goals is a skilful way to develop a guide and a roadmap to success. It is a basis of where we have to start and what plans and actions should be taken in order to reach what we want to achieve. If we have properly set plans, then we have to find adequate strategies to implement so that we can monitor whether we are on track or not.

Why do we need to set our goals? If we have goals, then we have something to look forward to, something to gauge our progress and keep the motivation to achieve our dreams. It sets the direction and whenever we feel weary and astray, our goals can remind us that we need faith to keep us on track with our greater purpose. So, how can we set our goals? There are many ways where we can develop our goals in any aspect of our life. Let me cite a concept called SMART goals, which was developed in 1981 by George Doran, Arthur Miller and James Cunningham. According to this model, SMART stands for Specific, Measurable, Achievable, Realistic and Timely. This is mostly applied to organizational goals or business-related objectives. It can be applied to personal goals as well. We can also explore from a wide array of resources that we can utilize and there is no fundamental equation in setting up our goals. It is all up to us to make our own plans with our own timeline and set of matrices to monitor our progress.

Let me give you a personal example of setting a SMART goal and how I was able to achieve it. Years ago, I took an Estidama-Pearl Qualified Professional (PQP) Certification exam in Abu Dhabi. It is a rating system for buildings encompassing the pillars of sustainability, which include environmental, economic, cultural and social aspects. I had to study the material for one month while working. The passing score to become a PQP was 70%, but I set an ambitious goal to become a certified PQP after one month of self-study with a score of 100%. What I did was focus on my goal and implement my strategies to study every day covering specific sections. I cut off social media and other distractions. My online exposure was only to video calls with my family, no TV, no other reading materials, and no extra-curricular activities for one month except work and studying for that period of time. With unfavourable irony, some other friends would laugh at me as to why I was seemingly a 'killjoy', but I just stuck to my goal and kept implementing my strategies every single day. There were days that I would feel I would not be able to hit my target, but I would console myself with the fact that if 100% is not achievable, then it might just go down to 98%. But with God's grace, my consistency and my positive mindset, I obtained a 100% score. This is not to brag, but it was rewarding and useful in upgrading my position in the field of environmental and sustainability.

The most important thing is we have our plans set. This is the roadmap that we follow as we traverse that long winding road to success. And in our journey we lift everything to our Creator for guidance, strength and the willpower to sustain us until we accomplish the desired results from our endeavors.

Take Actions

Making a plan is one thing, and translating that plan into action is an essential step in reaching our dreams and aspirations. A plan without action is just commensurate to an empty promise without taking responsibility to make things happen. An action requires hard work according to whatever plan we have established. And for us to attain the desired outcome, we need to be consistent in our actions. Although there may be times that our energy withers, we have to be reminded and reflect on our vision and not depend on feelings or emotions.

It is totally alright to go slow and even stumble at times, for as long as we won't give up our ambitions. Be it for personal, relationship or professional goals, slow and steady progress is better than quitting. When we seem to falter and lose motivation, we have to excite that zeal to continue moving forward. We may take a pause, reflect, and engage in self-introspection every time we experience setbacks, but quitting and giving up on our dreams is never an option.

After crafting our plans, if we just sit and watch things unfold, nothing will happen. Indolence will never get us somewhere. Our time is precious, and we need to keep going. Even tiny steps at a time will spell a significant difference in keeping up with what we aspire for. Consistent actions anchored in the right direction and attitude are essential if we want to achieve something.

Commitment and Discipline

When we commit our plans to God, we also take the ownership to stay committed in taking actions and consistently working on it. Commitment entails a strong determination to stay on course at all cost without regress, not being swayed by any discouragement. It means if we are tasked to undertake some activities, we do it without conditions and whatever it takes, we won't abandon the task.

If we work on something and we set our target, we need the right discipline to stay on track with our plans and actions. Discipline is needed to have consistent actions every day directed towards our goals. If we want to achieve our ambitions, sacrifices have to be made. For example, from an OFW perspective, since we made the decision to take this unique challenge to improve our life in many ways, then we need to have a deep commitment and stay disciplined so that no matter what happens, we will never give up until we see the desired results.

Then how can we do it? Staying committed requires us to stay connected with our anchor. A strong connection with our biggest WHY, our purpose in taking such endeavours. Commitment also requires an alignment with other positive traits as well as an awareness that we have to dedicate our time, efforts and resources to the implementation of our established plans.

Delayed Gratification

If you were given a choice, which one would you choose – enjoy now and sacrifice later or sacrifice now and enjoy later? I bet many of us will opt for the latter. We have to embrace the concept of delayed gratification, which means sacrificing first and enjoying it in the long run. We often heard this phrase during our university days. If we want to excel and accomplish our goal, we need to focus on that and avoid distractions or unnecessary activities that do not contribute to our goals. As human beings, it is innate in our character to celebrate our victories and enjoy. But delayed gratification would mean not being able to give in to temporary or instant enjoyment and just continue to work hard until we accomplish something that would make a difference in our lives.

Delayed gratification is not depriving ourselves but looking forward to a bigger reward with a positive perspective that self-sacrifice is part and parcel among the requisites as we journey to success. Sometimes, if we accede to instant gratification, it may become destructive, and we may lose sight of the bigger picture in working towards the penultimate fulfilment of our dreams.

Failure is Part of Success

When we do something or venture into anything, we are subjected to many challenges. Sometimes, when things get rough, we perceive that we are doomed to fail. But failure is part of our journey to success. We are not impeccable, we commit mistakes and have blind spots. When we don't achieve our goals, it doesn't necessarily mean that we fail. We just need realignment and re-evaluation of our strategies to see why things didn't happen as expected.

If we fail, it is a reminder and awakening that we need to do something and upscale our efforts. There is no failure in the real sense if we learn lessons from every setback. We have to reflect on lessons and always look at things with a positive outlook, thinking that they happen for good reasons. It is up to us to pick ourselves up with optimism that we need to rise anew, amplified with lessons from our failures. Failure is not a permanent state, if we have perseverance armed with renewed commitment and hard work, we will certainly bounce back and come out better.

The climb to success is strenuous and it requires perseverance and untainted commitment. If we fail and keep trying, then whatever adversities that would confront us will not matter anymore. The only thing in mind is our belief and hope to clinch the success we aim for.

A concrete example of bouncing back to recovery is that of a fellow OFW friend. Due to many problems, failures and difficult situations, he was downtrodden, depressed and lost hope. He was swamped by many issues in life and was on the brink of losing his mind due to health concerns and depression. With strong faith and determination, he was enlightened and realized that he needed to bounce back for himself and those who depend on him. He heeded my advice and started putting the broken pieces together and slowly working towards recovery. He is still struggling, but at least he is slowly progressing and change his perspectives. We have to realize that it is not yet too late, even if we fail big time. As long as we don't give up, there is always hope that things will get better.

Fulfillment in Helping Others

Extending help to other people is good, but we need to help ourselves first. When we achieve something, fulfilment is not only felt within us but there is also greater fulfilment when we can influence others to do better. Helping other people makes us feel better and gives us a sense of gratification. Extending help can be done in many ways. It can be through material things, financial services, or other benevolent actions that can benefit the recipient. When we are capable and it gives us pleasure, then we can propagate love and kindness as much as we can.

Encouraging and empowering others through our advice and words of wisdom from our experiences, especially for those who are in depressing situations, is a vital form of fulfilment. If we can lift up the spirits of those who are heavily burdened or with undesirable plight, it can make their day a bit better and help them to regain hope. Motivating others doesn't require huge efforts and big things. We can extend help in our own little ways; even our small gestures can make a difference in the lives of other people around us.

Propagating kindness and compassion is not limited to family or those within our close circle. We can be generous to a community that needs our services and voluntary work as well. In times of crisis and struggle, we can reach out to charitable organizations and extend some help. Being contributory to the greater cause of touching other people's lives is a sense of remarkable achievement.

Continually Moving Forward Towards Our Dreams

What does it take to achieve your dreams? The journey to success follows no one particular path. We can always recreate our strategies tailored to our situation. We can define our own paths and working towards our goals doesn't imply forgetting and fully detaching ourselves from vulnerabilities, but just employing a shield to always go beyond trials to better our life.

Despite the doom and gloom in our lives, there are many things to be grateful and happy about, and we should not stop from living and fulfilling our lives. Personally, I have come to terms with the fact that we don't need to strive hard for that willpower, for it lies within us. We just have to awaken our sensibilities so that we have our unique ability to harness that power. For example, over the years, I have been dreaming of writing my own book. I wanted my name to be an Author. With God's blessings, I am now making my dream come true.

From the perspective of OFWs striving to make a living thousands of miles away from home, it is imperative to realize that we should always find power and guidance from the Lord in fighting our battles from a distance. We should not succumb to defeat and depression because we can always find hope, inner strength and the fixity of purpose to move forward towards achieving our dreams.

We journey through the rough patches of discovering ourselves armed with the right purpose and positive mindset, but we can weather any obstacle that comes our way and never stop yearning for continual improvement. The self-realization that we have to unlock the power makes us appreciate our lives with the end goal of making a difference in the lives of many.

Personally, I have been through a mountain of problems and unfortunate incidents. For some days, I was defeated by the power of bad intentions. But I have learned to be resilient and regrets cannot help undo what has happened. On those occasions, I seemed to be powerless, but it paved the way to strengthen my connection to that greater Divine power for renewed strength and protection. I have realized that I can only redeem myself by moving forward, keeping the lessons and praying that God will give me the power to regain what is lost.

In our journey, we may stumble and feel deeply crushed at times. But if we cling to that inner power, then no matter how often our problems show up as obstacles in our path, we can always make our way towards achieving our dreams. Let us continue to dream big, work hard on the right path, and never lose grip and sight of that purpose in making a difference. In the end, we always look forward with a gratifying spirit as we continue to marvel at everything about life in the essence of achieving a fulfilled and happy life.

The Essence of Having a Mentor

In life, we are continuously learning from other people, especially from mentors. But who needs a mentor? Let us take an analogy in the field of sports. Many, if not the majority, are inclined to sports. For instance, Filipinos are fond of basketball in terms of sports. We either play it in our community or in schools or some have gone into professional games in this arena.

Let us take one example of a top and famous basketball achiever, Michael Jordan. Since his early days in this career, he has been guided by a Coach who has mentored him in terms of techniques and winning strategies, including personal development, to prepare him for rigorous training and actual challenges. Undoubtedly, he is an icon with unparalleled accolades and recognition; he is truly an unmatched champion. But it was not all about winning. He has worked hard and toiled with incomparable work ethics, guided by an excellent coach and an untainted goal to get better and better every day until he seized the phenomenal achievements.

It is in this light that in life, we also need mentors to inculcate much-needed lessons and implore guidance as we journey towards achieving our goals. I have my mentors whom I seek professional opinion and guidance when I have confusion and ambivalent dispositions. This helps me widen my reach and become more astute in my field.

On a personal aspect, I have realized that connecting to the right mentor has fortified my knowledge and capabilities and amplified my life in moving with a positive perspective to continually work on my goals. When I reawakened my interest in realizing my dream of becoming an Author, I discovered my limiting beliefs and stuck to the myths that it is indeed very difficult and not possible. However, my mentor has paved the way towards my realization that the possibility is in my hands if I believe that writing is a God-given talent and I have the power to unleash my potential.

The lessons I have learned from mentors have changed my perspective in a positive and productive way. I have learned to wane away from negativity and self-doubt, creating a space to embrace positivity and optimism to work towards my life goals. Over the years, I have been in desolation and discouragement. However, I realized that there is a power within me to have a paradigm shift in my belief system, to leave behind what I have been accustomed to that has dragged me down.

We can have mentors and advisors who can influence and impact positively in our life. Some life-changing decisions can be ignited when we have people who can supplement and harmonize the pieces needed towards the right direction. As a Filipino migrant worker, I have been through many adversities and have mustered strength to overcome them with grit and positivity.

Having gone through the same quandary as other OFWs, I can say that we connect with each other in a community anchored with the greatest mentor – the Divine power, where we generate positive impact and inspiration. In doing so, we can tap the hidden power within us geared towards meaningful transformation to become better versions of ourselves. Certainly, we can achieve our dreams and genuinely transcend beneficial impacts on other OFWs, our families, and other people's lives.

Keep moving forward, keep that vision alive, keep dreaming, keep working hard towards the realization of your dreams and make a difference in the lives of others.

About the Book

As human beings, we are always soaked into several challenges in life. Sometimes, we become frail, discouraged and unable to function well in the face of adversity. This comes in some confusing situations when we often doubt our abilities and lose hope. But if we know who we are, what we want and our aspirations, then we can realize that life is precious and worth living.

We all need deep and profound inspiration to get through. Being an OFW for a considerable period of time, it finally descended upon me that I have to continually work towards the realization of my dreams despite challenging situations. I've decided to write this book on how I hurdled insurmountable challenges and limiting beliefs. However gloomy the journey may be, I want to share my experiences and perspectives with the hope of touching the lives of those in the same predicament as mine. It is with this optimistic visualization of harnessing the hidden power within us to connect to that ultimate Divine power in order to overcome obstacles and come out better versions of ourselves.

For OFWs and their families, this book might be instrumental in changing your perspectives in life, for it is my fervent hope and prayer that I can be able to sow some inspiration. I proceed to envisage a realization—in the end, choosing a different path leaves behind many lessons, and we have ample reasons to move forward and grow into a better person.

We are on a journey laden with trials and obstacles, yet we come out stronger. Let us stay connected in a community where positivity and optimism dominate. The concepts and perspectives I have presented in this book can be instrumental in stimulating inspiration to achieve our dreams of a happy and fulfilled life.

About the Author

Eva Magalay Barientos is an Overseas Filipino Worker (OFW) in Dubai, UAE; an Engineer by profession and gained numerous professional certifications in Environment and Sustainability. She has taken a different path to pursue her dreams and aspirations in life and was able to hurdle many challenges as an OFW. In the pursuit of making a difference in the lives of her loved ones, she has painstakingly moved forward and overcome obstacles along the way.

She resolutely believes that education is powerful tool to improve life and that learning is a continuous process to fortify our arsenal, both personally and professionally. She also believes that our capabilities blended with the right attitude and God's providence are key drivers in achieving our dreams.

She embraces simplicity as a way of life. She has the passion of sharing knowledge and advices to many friends and other people needing her help. She has been incessantly dreaming of creating an impact to other people by sharing inspiration through her many defeats and victories.

You can connect to Eva:

Email: evabarientosf2024@gmail.com

9 789360 062255